MY FATHERS' FATHERS:

The History of the Jacks Family in America from 1667

MY FATHERS' FATHERS:

The History of the Jacks Family in America from 1667

by

James Joseph Jacks

GA

Geron & Associates

2011

IV

A Geron & Associates book from Watercress Press
San Antonio, Texas
www.watercresspress.com

Book design by Fishead Design Studio & Microgallery
www.fisheadproductions.com

ISBN 934955-86-7

CONTENTS

ILLUSTRATIONS

MY FATHERS' FATHERS:

The History of the Jacks Family in America from 1667

PREFACE

When I began work on this book, I had one simple objective . . . to breathe life into the names of my ancestors. For decades they were fading ink on ageing sheets of paper, stored in never-opened trunks. I was determined to discover enough about them, and transform as many as possible – and as much as possible – into real people.

When I was 18, I knew none of my father's fathers names; absolutely none. When I was 48, nothing had changed; while I was the caretaker of an amazing genealogical work assembled by my father's sister Ruth, it remained for decades as an unread and decaying stack of papers. When I was 58, I had begun wondering about my ancestors, but my career insured there was no time for the needed research. Now I'm 68 and well aware of my mortality. I'm driven to learn all I can and preserve our Jacks family history. Hopefully this same curiosity and passion will someday manifest itself in some of my descendents. Perhaps one of them might even decide to write a continuation.

Jone Jacks was born somewhere in England around 1640, and came to America around 1667 as an indentured servant. From his line came gentlemen farmers and plantation owners, Revolutionary War patriots, shoemakers, Confederate soldiers, poor farmers, large successful farmers, restaurant owners, and countless others. There is no way Jone Jacks could have envisioned this vast array of descendents.

Prior to beginning this book, I could see the individual family stories only as one sees through the faintness of twilight.

They were, for the most part, blurry unconnected dots. As my research progressed, the dots became linked and the names became real people. As I studied the area and times in which they lived I began to see that my ancestors helped build the most famous and powerful nation the world has ever known. They were right in the thick of it all. My forefathers had been here 100 years before the signing of the Declaration of Independence. Several fought as patriots in the American Revolution. They were neighbors of Daniel Boone. They were on the leading edge of many mass migrations to the West that are recounted in American history.

I chose not to weight this book down with countless academic footnotes. This is a personal story of real people, our Jacks family and the strong, brave frontier women they married. This is their story. We should be proud of them. This is our story.

My very special thanks to my aunt, Ruth Nolan Jacks Brocker, who spent hours sharing her memories with me and who graciously gave me a copy of our family's genealogy records. Also special thanks to her son, historian and author James H. Jacks-Brocker, for his help researching our Civil War family history, and to my beloved cousin James Raymond McDonald, son of my father's sister Una Lee Jacks McDonald, for his help with old photos and newspaper articles.

And finally to my wife Danine and to my children for their support and encouragement; especially to Danine for tolerating my extended periods of seclusion during the research and writing.

James Joseph Jacks
Son of James Martin Jacks and
direct descendent of Jone Jacks

21 June 2011
Johnson City, Texas

CHAPTER 1

JONE JACKS

Born About 1643 in England – Date of Death Unknown

Who Was the Father of Thomas Jacks?

Our family line prior to Thomas Jacks becomes blurry. Some family researchers believe the father of Thomas could have been an immigrant to the American colonies named Richard Jacks. Richard, like Jone, was born in England somewhere between 1619 and 1648. Richard is believed to have married a lady named Mary Agnes Coffley. Richard is believed to have come from England to Massachusetts about 1635. Jone Jacks, the person most researchers believe to be the most viable candidate, seems to have had a much more colorful past. This is what we know about Jone.

The Father of Us All

Legend says Jone began his voyage to the American Colonies in the 1660s as a stowaway aboard a ship from England that became crippled due to high winds, and ran aground on islands – probably the Outer Hebrides, just off the coast of England. This legend says Jone, after some delay, secured passage again; this time arriving successfully in the colonies. There is a record of a sailor named Jon Jacks arriving in the port of Boston on the Rob McCurdy-owned sloop *Endeavour*, from Halifax, England.

This is possibly our ancestor Jone Jacks. We do know that upon arrival Jone entered into an indentured servant contract.

Indentured servant contracts were very popular during this period because of the extremely high demand for labor in the colonies. Tobacco farming – which was quite labor-intensive – accounted for most of the demand but by no means all. Many professions and trades needed a workforce, and demand was growing faster than the population of the colonies. A little-known aspect of this period in American history is that African slaves were only a fraction of the labor force used to grow tobacco. Not only was the slave trade flourishing in the Americas, but there was also a high demand for persons willing to come to the colonies to work for a period of years, as outlined in a contract. In addition, England discovered it could empty its prisons by sending prisoners to America to be sold at auction. They were sold for certain periods of time, depending on their crime, and their price was much cheaper than a regular African slave or that of an indentured servant.

Indentured servant contracts were generally from four to seven years, depending on their skill, age, and general health. Sometimes a contract could be struck with an individual before leaving England, but generally they were purchased by middlemen, transported to America, and sold by the middlemen at action. The middlemen would then be able to recover the cost of transporting the individual (about £4 Sterling) and make a profit. A convict's contract, on the other hand, was quite different and depended on the crime they were convicted of. A convict could receive one of three terms: seven years, fourteen years, or banishment for life (74, 24, and 2 percent of the total convicts shipped, respectively).

Convicts were a bargain, when compared with indentured servants and slaves. They served almost twice the time of indentured servants. Most indentured servant contracts contained a freedom dues clause; sometimes a small parcel of land, some tools and seed, etc, or in the case of a tradesman, some cash, some clothes, and other benefits. So for the harsh plantation work, the most sought-after were convicts. A convict could be purchased for £12-£15 Sterling, while a male slave in good health could cost £50.

So after one false start, young Jone Jacks arrived in America and entered into an indentured servant contract with a ship-builder or "master of transportance" named Richard F. Halleyne, for a period of seven years. Under this contract, he could expect to learn the shipbuilding trade, and at the end of his obligation, receive a severance pay. Often this also included a set of clothes. The entire Chesapeake Bay area depended on ships to transport goods to and from the colonies. No doubt Jone would be able to find work, either as a sailor or in his new trade as shipbuilder. It is believed that Jone began his contract with Richard Halleyne in 1667, the year of his arrival.

Why Did Jone Leave England

Many might be tempted to ask why a young man would leave his homeland, come across the ocean to a country where he presumably knew no one, and commit to work for a man he did not know, and in a profession he probably knew little if anything about. The answers to these questions almost certainly lie in the economic, political, and religious conditions in England at the time. These were times of significant change. Religious struggles were taking place between the Catholic Church, the Church of England, and the "reformed" groups such as the Puritans. Land and tax struggles were ongoing between the emerging "gentry" class and the older established nobility. King Charles I was trying to keep alive the convenient doctrine of the "divine right of kings," which basically held that the king answered only to God. The period of 1642-1651 saw what history would later call the English Civil War. This event would eventually lead to the beheading of Charles I, the exile of his son, Charles II, the replacement of the English monarchy, and a significant loss of power for the Church of England. If you were not born into a noble family, did not belong to the land-owning class, or have a successful in-demand craft, you would probably find yourself – as most in England did at the time – in a class of landless laborers with a miserable life and little hope for advancement.

Stories had been filtering back to England for years about the opportunities awaiting those who would be brave enough to risk all and come to the new American colonies. Almost certainly, young Jone Jacks heard this call and responded. He would not have been alone. Many were leaving England for the colonies for just this same reason, so making the decision to come would have been less difficult for Jone, as he would have been among many young Englishmen doing exactly the same thing.

What Did Jone Find when he Arrived?

Life in the American colonies in the 1660s and 1670s was – in many ways – uninviting. Among the new immigrants during this period, men outnumbered women five to two, and death before age fifty was common. Some sources say it was not until the year 1680 that live births equaled deaths and the population of the colonies began to sustain itself. Most arriving in the colony were young and single. About 75% of the arriving immi-grants were indentured servants. However, many also arrived in the area without indenture and later secured a contract on their own to a desirable person, in exchange for learning a trade. An example of an early indentured contract reads as follows: "Learn to read and learn the trade of carpentry. Bound till the age of 21. At expiration of contract one cow and one calf."

Many like Jone were older when they entered into a

contract, and thus they tended to marry later in life, after having completed the terms of their contract. However, because of the shortage of unmarried women, many never married. Jone probably arrived in America around the age of 24 and immediately thereafter (because of the necessity of feeding himself) found the shipbuilder Richard Halleyne and went to work for him. Jone would then have been about 31 when he finished his contract to the shipbuilder. He likely married soon afterwards. Assuming John entered his seven-year contract with Richard Halleyne in 1667, he would have finished it in 1674 and likely married immediately upon finishing his contract. His son, Thomas Jacks, Sr., was born between 1675 (the year following the completion of his contract) and 1684. We are not sure who Jone married.

What profession Jone followed after finishing his indentured contract with Richard Halleyne is also not known. Shipbuilding was a major industry in the Chesapeake Bay area, so Jone could have easily continued working for Halleyne, joined a competitor, or even gone into the business for himself. Both fishing and transporting tobacco created significant demand for the building and repair of ships. One reason for the success of the shipbuilding industry in the Chesapeake Bay area was the availability of timber throughout the area, a resource that had been largely depleted in England. Historical records indicate one of the most frequent requests from the colonies to England was for those trained in shipbuilding. Not only was the demand for ships and boats high, but the huge needs of the large tobacco plantations kept a constant strain on the manpower supply available to the shipbuilders. Because Jone's son Thomas was listed primarily as a shoemaker, we might assume Thomas did not grow up on his father's tobacco plantation.

Jone's Son Thomas

Thomas Jacks (Sr.) was born between 1675 and 1684, probably on or very near the Chesapeake Bay, in Somerset County, Maryland. Assuming Jone married soon after finishing his contract with Halleyne, his son was probably born about 1675. As stated earlier, Jone would have been around 31 years old at that time. Life expectancy of those who came to the colonies as indentured servants was not very long. Records indicate most did not live much beyond age 50. The women died closer to age 40, and tended to marry younger, as there were about five men to every two women in this early period. We don't know when he died, but if Jone and his wife fell into the above statistics, by the time Thomas reached about 21 years of age, both his mother and father would have been dead. Court records from the time indicate orphans were a significant social problem. Children and siblings were frequently brought into "orphan's court" and assigned to families till they reached certain ages, either into indentured agreements, or simply as orphans. Historians calculate that during this early period in the colonies, 75% of children had lost at least one parent before the age of 21 and 33% had lost both parents by that time.

Life expectancy back in England was longer, so why did people like Jone leave England, risk an ocean crossing, and indenture themselves for seven years to come live in the American colonies? The answer is complex and yet simple. If they chose to remain in England, they would die in the class into which they were born. In America, they had the opportunity to work themselves out of poverty. They had a real possibility to become landowners, something virtually impossible for someone like Jone had he chosen to remain in England.

The Jacks Family before America (Huguenot, English, Scot, or What?)

The mist of time obscures our past before Jone. One of the most interesting and widely-accepted theories relating to who we are and from whence we came is the Huguenot connection. Many believe that the Jacks came directly to America from France after the Revocation of the Edict of Nantes. They believe our name is the Anglicization of Jacques or Jacque. History bears this out to some extent – but Jone Jacks and his son Thomas were already in the colonies before the revocation of the Edict of Nantes. That edict was issued in 1598 by Henry IV of France, and subsequently revoked by his grandson Louis XIV in 1685. The original purpose of the edict was to provide protection and civil rights to those Calvinist Protestants, also referred to as Huguenots. Officially they were members of the Protestant Reformed Church of France. The Huguenots suffered extreme persecution in France by the Catholic Church and many were massacred during a period of hostilities known as the French Wars of Religion. The Edict of Nantes basically brought a period of some tranquility for the Huguenots, but when the edict was revoked many French Protestants fled across the channel to England and Scotland, as well as to Switzerland, Holland, Prussia, Germany, and even to South Africa. Some figures claim as many as 400,000 Huguenots fled France. But as we see, Jone is found – via his indentured servant contract – already in Maryland by 1667, significantly before the 1685 Revocation. Son Thomas may also have been born before the Revocation.

This does not preclude Jone Jacks from being of French Protestant lineage, however. It simply seems to indicate he could not have come to America directly from France. Religious persecution was so strong prior to the Revocation of the Edict of Nantes that many had already left France for England and Scotland. Even during the "protection" afforded by the edict many atrocities were committed against these French Protestants. Thus, it is entirely possible some of them named Jacques or Jacque were Jone's ancestors. However, the Anglicization of the French Jacques or Jacque into Jacks is believed to have begun much earlier . . . most family historians believe about the time of the Norman Conquest after 1066. The Normans lived in the northern part of France. With their victory over the English came huge challenges in maintaining control over the vast English territory they had just conquered. One approach the Normans took was encouraging mass immigration of those previously living in Normandy, as well as French citizens from other provinces outside Normandy. With this massive wave of French immigrants into England, almost certainly came some Jacks ancestors around the year 1066. Their names would have slowly changed from Jacques and Jacque, to Jake, Jacke, Jeke, Jack, and finally Jacks. Recorded use of the surname Jacke in England dates back as early as 1302 and Jacks is recorded in 1577. This means that when the Huguenots arrived in England, their new name was already well established. They were Jacques or Jacque in France but in their country of refuge, in England or Scotland, they would be called Jack or Jacks. The pronunciation is almost identical.

As for the Jacks roots in Scotland, they don't seem to be very significant. According to *Ancestry.com's* extensive databases, in the year 1841, only 31 Jacks families were reported living in Scotland. By contrast, the 1840 U.S. Census shows 61 Jacks families living in the United States. The 1891 census of England and Wales showed 754 Jacks families. Clearly the largest concentration of Jacks families was in England and Wales. To demonstrate how uncommon our Jacks name is, the 1891 census for England and Wales showed 349,541 Jones surnames.

The Huguenot Surprise

While sifting through volumes of *Ancestry.com* statistics, I was struck by some undeniable figures from the "New York Passenger Lists 1820-1957." The Jacks immigrants were sorted by "top places of origin." Listed from countries with the most

Jacks immigrants to the least, the countries were as follows: Germany, Prussia, England, Hungary, Germanic Alsace-Lorraine, and Poland. Where did the Huguenots go when fleeing France? To these same countries. About 50,000 Walloon (French-speaking Belgians) and Huguenots fled to England. From there an estimated 10,000 moved on to Ireland. They were heavily concentrated in the Canterbury area which was at the time a center for Calvinists. Many of these Huguenots were or became weavers and lace makers.

By the mid 1600s Huguenots were arriving in the American colonies in significant numbers also. As stated above, they were primarily coming from the countries where they had gone after fleeing France. Many settled in New Netherland, New Amsterdam, New Platz, New Rochelle, Staten Island, and other areas of New York. Others settled in Pennsylvania and integrated into the existing German communities.

Browsing the Jacks passenger lists revealed John Jacks was by far the most common name. Thomas, Robert, and Nicholas were also common. It was like looking at my family tree, and yet these people were born long after Jone, Thomas, and John. Nicholas was extremely common from the German immigrants, and William, John, and Robert among the English. Could many of these Jacks immigrants have been descendents of the Huguenot refugees of France? Was Jone Jacks a descendent of one of the 50,000 French-speaking Belgians and Huguenots who fled to England?

Most of the Huguenots rapidly integrated and married into their surrounding communities and were eventually completely assimilated. Before this happened however, they left markers to insure their remembrance for posterity. Many historic landmarks in New York City are from the Huguenots. They also gave us Revolutionary War heroes Paul Revere, gun-powder maker E.I. du Pont, Jack Jouett who rode from Cuckoo Tavern to warn

Thomas Jefferson that a group of British solders under the command of Tarleton were coming to arrest him for "crimes against the king", and Declaration of Independence signer Henry Laurens. So while Jone Jacks did not come to America as a result of the Revocation of the Edict of Nantes, he could very well have been descended from those Huguenots who fled France prior to the Revocation.

The Jacks Family after Jone
Thomas Jacks Sr. about 1675-1756: Planter and early Anne Arundel County, Maryland, settler. Father of Thomas, Elizabeth, Barbara (Barbary), <u>Richard</u>, and Anne.

Richard James Jacks, 1713-1787: Planter and early resident of Anne Arundel County, Maryland, early settler of Rowan County, North Carolina. Father of Elizabeth, Thomas, Richard, Reuben, <u>John Nicholas Sr.</u>, William (Martin), Barbara, Nancy, Rachel, and Edward.

John Nicholas Jacks Sr.: about 1740 – about 1826. Planter and Revolutionary War patriot (North Carolina Militia). Neighbor of Daniel Boone, later early settler in Kentucky. Father of John <u>Nicholas Jr.</u>, Richard Marion, Thomas, Mary (Polly), Anna, William Milton, and Tobitha.

John Nicholas Jacks Jr.: about 1770 – after 1851. Farmer, active in founding frontier Baptist churches in Kentucky and Alabama. One of the first residents of Jefferson County, Alabama, site of modern-day Birmingham. Father of Thomas, Penelope, James Keen, Lucy, John Greenberry, Mary (Polly), Elizabeth, <u>Nicholas</u>, Sarah Labony (Sabaray), George G. (Columbus), Richard Martin or William Martin.

Nicholas Jacks: about 1804 – between 1880 and 1906. Farmer, tanner, early resident of Jefferson County, Alabama, lived in

Chickasaw County, Mississippi, and Montgomery County, Arkansas. Father of <u>Larkin Harrison</u>, William Thompson, John Martin, Mary Ann (Polly), James Keene, Nancy Jane, Elizabeth (Eliza), Mariah Frances, Sarah Elizabeth, Harriet Amanda (Mandy), Lucinda, Abraham Nicholas, and Melinda Margaret.

Larkin Harrison Jacks: 1826-1908. Farmer, and Confederate States of America patriot. Early resident of Lincoln County, Arkansas. Father of Nancy Jane, Lydia Francis, Sarah Elizabeth, <u>James Martin</u>, William Robert (Bob), John Nicholas, and Martin Andrew.

James Martin Jacks: 1852-1923. Farmer and founding member of Harmony Missionary Baptist Church, Jefferson County, Arkansas. Father of seventeen children: Calvin James, <u>Charles Larkin</u>, Albert, Cora Amanda, Sarah, William Claudis, Thomas Grover, and Andrew Douglas by first wife Amanda (Mandy) Bailey. By second wife Sarah Lucinda Wortham: Jennie Bell, Edgar Austin, Bertha Leona, Henry Floyd, May or Mary, Fred Nicholas, Arthur Garland, Ruby, and Bessie Ione.

Charles Larkin Jacks, 1875-1914. Restaurant owner. Father of Claude Willis, Una Lee, Ruth, and <u>James Martin</u>.

James Martin Jacks, 1909-1976. Manager Lone Star Gas Company. Father of <u>James Joseph</u> and Camille.

James Joseph Jacks, 1943 – Living. Pilot and Aviation Executive. Father of Jason Jerome, Jennifer Joelle, Martin Norodom, and Michael Sisowath.

According to *Ancestry.com*'s computer analysis, based on the 1920 U.S. Census, there were 922 Jacks families in America.

Certainly they are not all descendents of our ancestor Jone. Jone's descendents became farmers and tanners, solders and shoemakers, pilots and preachers and everything in between. One was in debtor's prison, one was an indentured servant, some owned slaves. Several Jacks fought in the American Revolution – some were Jone's descendents. Several fought in the Civil War; many of these were also Jone's descendents. Sixty-four men with the surname of Jacks fought for the Union and eighty-two fought for the Confederacy. While we have no way of knowing how many of them were our direct ancestors, we know there were many.

Certainly Jone Jacks would be amazed to see all his descendents today. He could never have known the results of his brave decision to say goodbye to those he knew in England and risk a trans-Atlantic voyage, followed by seven years of indentured servitude. He would be truly amazed.

CHAPTER 2

THOMAS JACKS SR.

About 1675 - 25 October 1756

Our First Ancestor Born in America – Anne Arundel County, Maryland

Thomas Jacks is believed to be the son of an Englishman named Jone Jacks, and was probably born about 1675 in Anne Arundel County, Maryland. Thomas led an interesting and colorful life. He was a shoemaker or "cordwainer" by trade; that term as used in the old Maryland documents specifically refers to one who made fine leather shoes from soft expensive leather, as opposed to a cobbler who made or repaired less refined shoes. Later, it appears Thomas tried his luck at farming as he is in some places also referred to as a planter. Thomas was a member of the Church of England.

Elizabeth Gardner Powell Walters Jacks

On 9 November 1704, Thomas Jacks married the twice-widowed Elizabeth Gardner, daughter of Luke and Monica Gardner. Elizabeth had first married John Powell on 20 July 1693. They had two children: John Powell Jr. and Joseph. About 1695, after only about two years of marriage, John Powell died. His neighbor Thomas Jacks probably attended the funeral. The

Powell place was located on the banks of the Severn River, which flows into Chesapeake Bay near Annapolis.

Shortly afterwards, the widowed Elizabeth Powell married Christopher Walters on 16 February 1696 at All Hallows Parish, Anne Arundel County, Maryland. This was only about two and a half years after she married her first husband John Powell. Some report Christopher Walters was in the colonial military service. On 16 August 1698 Elizabeth had her third child, son Christopher Jr., and on 8 February 1701, her fourth child and first daughter, Ann, was born. Then on 22 May 1703 her second husband, Christopher Walters, died. Thomas Jacks could have attended this funeral also. From her second husband, Elizabeth inherited a large plantation called Greenfield.

About seventeen months later, on 9 November 1704, Elizabeth Gardner Powell Walters married her neighbor Thomas Jacks. Like her marriage to Christopher Walters, this marriage also took place in All Hallows Parish and is recorded in Marriage Book 1-AA on page 65.

Thomas and Elizabeth Begin Their Life Together

About three months after their marriage, Thomas purchased "100 acres called 'Gentill Craft' being part of the tract called Roper Grey," from William Roper for 100 pounds. This transaction was recorded on 23 July 1706. The following year, on 4 August 1706, Elizabeth had her fifth child and her first with husband Thomas. The child was a son and they named him Thomas. In Boston of that same year, Benjamin Franklin was born.

On 10 July 1707, Thomas and Elizabeth appear in the Anne Arundel County records as part of the will (testers) of John Sellman of Anne Arundel County.

On 6 December 1707, less than three years after Thomas purchased Gentile Craft (note different spellings), the following transaction is recorded: Anne Arundel County, Maryland, Bk WT 2, p.603 "Thomas Jacks of Anne Arundel, cordwainer, and Elizabeth, his wife sold 100 acres for 22 pounds. Thomas signed his name with his mark 'T' and Elizabeth, her mark 'A'". They sold to Amos Garrett. This was recorded on 8 April 1708. Note they paid 100 pounds for the tract of land and sold it for 22 pounds. This is a significant loss and probably indicates financial difficulties or that different currencies were used on the transactions.

On 27 June 1708, Thomas and Elizabeth had their second child (sixth child for Elizabeth), a daughter they named Elizabeth. Elizabeth the daughter would die early in life and her four children would be raised by Thomas and his wife Elizabeth.

A Runaway Servant

An interesting court proceeding is recorded in 1708 in the Anne Arundel County March court records. It appears Thomas had an indentured servant named John Hammond. Apparently, John tired of life with Thomas and decided to take off for awhile. From the way the account reads, it appears John's return might not have been voluntarily. The report is as follows: "Thomas Jacks' servant, John Hammond, returned after running away. Was ordered to serve his master for 10 months to repay the 920 pounds of tobacco expended in taking him up, and given 73 days more for the runaway time."

In addition to this interesting event, the record also brings to light some little-known aspects of life in the early colonies. Indentured servitude was a common way for people to earn passage to the colonies from England. It was very common in the Chesapeake Bay area. But in addition to this indentured servitude, there was an apprentice contract which generally offered much better terms. For an indentured servant, usually the main part of the contract was the length of service which could be extended for infractions, etc. For the apprentice contract, both parties had obligations, the master usually agreeing to provide, food, lodging, clothing, as well as training in his craft. The apprentice contract was usually considerably shorter than the indentured one and offered a much better life. Since Thomas was a cordwainer, it is more likely that John Hammond was an apprentice bound by an agreement while he learned the trade. But as we see, Thomas also was a planter so Hammond could have been working on the plantation. Another aspect of life during that period is that initially on the tobacco plantations indentured servants did most of the work. But as the number of indentured servant contracts began to drop, the number of African slaves increased. Also of significance is the use of tobacco as money. It was the most stable form of currency at that time in the Chesapeake colonies, and always had a value in exchange for gold. Even those living in towns planted small patches of tobacco, which they could exchange for tobacco transfer notes, which then could be used as currency at shops in town to purchase their commodities.

Three More Children for Thomas and Elizabeth— Barbara "Barbary," Richard James, and Ann

On 21 September 1712, Thomas and Elizabeth had their third child, daughter Barbara. Barely nine months later, on 7 June 1713, their fourth child, Richard James, was born, and about 1715, their last child, daughter Ann, was born, all in Anne Arundel County, Maryland.

While Thomas and Elizabeth's family was growing, events in the colonies and across the ocean were setting a course that few at the time would recognize for what they really were. In 1714, tea was first introduced from England to the colonies. In August of the same year, King George 1 would ascend to the British throne, succeeding Queen Anne. In 1718 the French

founded New Orleans. Small tobacco farmers like Thomas were
being replaced by larger and larger tobacco plantations, which
were facilitated by increases in slave importation. British taxation of tobacco was rapidly climbing. While the wealthy seemed
to prosper, the vast majority at the bottom of the economic
strata languished in poverty, and each arriving ship brought new
economic refugees from England to compete for the unskilled
jobs, or to join the huge ranks of indentured servants. There
was a growing discontent.

John Powell Jr.'s Death & Will – Joseph Powell's Death

John Powell Sr., Elizabeth Jacks' son by her first marriage,
died about 1695 and left a sizable inheritance to his son John
Powell Jr., who was raised by Thomas and Elizabeth. In John
Jr.'s will, he left his inheritance-"Powell's Inheritance"-to his
mother Elizabeth. John Powell Jr. died on 7 November 1715.
John Jr. would have been about 20 years of age at the time of his
death. Five months later, on 6 April 1716, John Powell Jr.'s will
is proved. John's mother, Elizabeth Jacks, inherited Powell's
Inheritance on the South River, for her lifetime. After her death
John Jr.'s brother Joseph and his heirs would inherit. Should
Joseph lack issue, said land is to pass to Richard Jacks, his half-
brother and his heirs. The wording of the record from this point
is unclear but it appears that John Jr. also left brother
Christopher Walters and half-brother Thomas Jacks and his two
half-sisters Elizabeth and Barbary or Barbara 200 acres each.

More Land Transactions – and a Lawsuit

On 24 April 1717, the Anne Arundel County, Maryland,
Deed Book (IB #2 p.380) records a sale from Benjamin Williams
of Anne Arundel County, a planter, to Thomas Jacks, of same, a
cordwainer. The transaction was far two tracts of land which
had been tied up in an estate. One tract of 100 acres was known

as Elk Thicket. The 26-acre tract was called Williams Addition.

Five months later, on 28 September 1717, the Anne Arundel County, Maryland, records show that a tract of 300 acres was surveyed for Thomas Jacks called Jack's Peacock in Baltimore County, located on the drafts of the main falls of the Patapsco River on the south side. A note says the land is now in Howard County, Maryland. The land was patented to Thomas Jacks on 6 August 1719. This probably came from the Maryland colonial government, and documented that Thomas had an interest in the land. Usually it was not until the patented land had been surveyed that the ownership became seriously defendable. The tract of land was probably about ten miles due west of the city of Baltimore. The document notes that Thomas then rented the land out, two hundred acres to Phillip Hammond, and 100 acres to Richard Snowden. Almost certainly this land was being used for growing tobacco.

In 1718 Thomas was called into court to answer charges of nonpayment of accounts by Gilbert Higginbotham. The charge says "divers goods, wares and merchandise" had been delivered to Jacks. He said that although Thomas had promised to pay several times, Thomas always defaulted. The sum of the delinquent account was 64 pounds, 15 shillings, and 3 pence. The settlement was delayed until June of 1719 when Thomas was ordered to pay 40 pounds current money to Higginbotham for his damages.

By 1720 the population of the colonies had reached 475,000. The largest city in the colonies was Boston with a population of about 12,000, followed by Philadelphia with 10,000, and New York with 7,000. By 1725 the population of black slaves had reached 75,000. Of every 100 persons in the colonies, sixteen were slaves.

On 3 February 1724, about seven years after Thomas had the 300-acre tract of land surveyed, he sold 200 acres of the parcel to a man in London named John Taylor for only five shillings. In the deed, Thomas was identified as a planter in Baltimore County. This may have been a "fire sale" as future court records suggest. In a probably unrelated court record of 15 August 1726, Joseph Powell transferred the inheritance he received from his brother John Jr. to his half-brother Richard, who was only 13 years old at the time.

On 14 November 1728, in Anne Arundel County, Maryland, we find an indenture or real estate transaction from Thomas Jacks of Anne Arundel County, cordwainer, to Richard Snowden, merchant, for 60 pounds for "all that 100 acres of land being the dwelling plantation of the said Thomas Jacks." Note that here Thomas is once again referred to as cordwainer or shoemaker, and not planter. Apparently this Richard Snowden to whom Thomas was previously renting the land agreed to purchase it from Thomas.

Debtor's Prison

In colonial America, being jailed for nonpayment of debts was not uncommon. The practice arrived in the colonies from England. Some famous Americans were in debtor's prisons. Declaration of Independence signers James Wilson and Robert Morris were both later incarcerated. Henry Lee III, better known as Light-Horse Harry Lee, a Revolutionary War general, former governor of Virginia, and father of Robert E. Lee, was reportedly imprisoned for debt between 1808 and 1809. One source states as many as 2,000 New Yorkers annually were put in debtor's prisons by the year 1816. So ancestor Thomas (whether Sr. or Jr.) was possibly just caught in an institution of the times as we shall see here. On 26 May 1730, Anne Arundel County, Maryland, records tell an interesting story; one Thomas Jacks and several others were in prison for their inability to repay debts. They petitioned the Maryland legislature for relief, claiming that if they remained in prison, they would never have the ability to repay their debts. The legislature, in response to the petition, enacted a bill and presented it to the governor on 30 June 1730. The bill provided for the debtors to transfer all their assets to the Sheriff of Anne Arundel County to be used by the sheriff to satisfy their debts. According to the bill, if they did this, they would be released within 20 days. On 16 July of 1730, Thomas Jacks, described as a shoemaker and languishing prisoner in the Anne Arundel County jail, transferred to the sheriff of Anne Arundel County, for the use of his creditors, all his rights in Powell's Inheritance. Attached to the indenture was a schedule of all the goods and chattels delivered by Thomas Jacks to the sheriff. Listed on the attachment of assets, are one old hammock, one old block bed, and one iron pot left in the prison containing about three gallons. Some researchers believe this was Thomas Jr. rather than Thomas Jacks Sr. However, for that to be true, Thomas Jr. would have had to be a shoemaker also. This would not have been uncommon. The Thomas Jr. theory probably stems from belief that Thomas Sr. did not directly have any ownership in the property Powell's Inheritance, whereas son Thomas Jr. did.

Raising Orphans

Anne Arundel County Court records of June 1736 page 445 states, "Thomas Jacks brings into court four orphan children, the issue of Robert Huit, deceased, in order to be bound out by this court and thereupon the said Jacks is ordered to take care of the said children until next court and that he then bring them to be bound out apprentices by the court and the said court agrees to pay the said Jacks for the keeping of them until then at the same rate as they usually give for the maintenance of orphans."

These four children are apparently Thomas and Elizabeth's grandchildren. Their second child, Elizabeth, born 27 June

1708, had married Robert Huit/Huett about 1725. Eleven years later court records indicate her husband Robert is dead. Depending on how it is read, it may indicate Elizabeth is also deceased. At the next court session in August 1736, court record book 1736 page 4, records "The court binds unto Thomas Jacks and Elizabeth his wife, Robert Huit, Jacob Huit, Edward Huit, and Hannah Huit, children of Robert and Elizabeth Huit, deceased, until they arrive to the age of 21 years the boys and 16 years the girl (Robert Huit being 10 years old the 2nd day of July last, Jacob Huit 8 years old the 17th of this instant, Edward Huit six years old the 2nd day of March last, and Hannah Huit 4 years old the 10th day of October next. In consideration whereof the said Thomas Jacks and Elizabeth his wife obligates themselves to find them sufficient meat, drink, washing clothing and lodging to give each of them a good suit of clothes at the expiration of their servitude, also their endeavor to learn them to read and write whereof it is considered by the justices here that the said Robert, Jacob, Edward, and Hannah serve the said Thomas Jacks and Elizabeth his wife the term afore said accordingly." A researcher's note says that at the end of the preceding it states, "Anne Arundel County Maryland Judgments 1702-1793." The researcher probably correctly believes that this would have been a special court for deserted and orphaned children.

Another Children Story (Or Maybe It's an Adult Story)

To say that Thomas was a friend of the court might not be exactly accurate, but he sure was familiar with the system. On 11 June 1745, poor Thomas, now age about 70, is back in court once more. It appears that one of his servants, a lady by the name of Mary Candis, had a child outside wedlock, which was significantly frowned upon in the colony at that time. The story goes like this: Anne Arundel Court of June 1745 page 313-314. "Mary Candis, a servant woman of Thomas Jacks, comes into court and confesses that she has a base-born child called Margaret aged about three years and submits to the court's judgment thereon. It is therefore considered by the Justices Court that the said Mary Candis for the offense aforesaid be taken by the Sheriff of Anne Arundel County to the public whipping post, and received on her bare back 5 lashes well laid on and the said Sheriff is commanded to do immediate execution of the judgment aforesaid and soon after returns and says that he hath performed the same. Thereupon the said Mary Candis is discharged, her master being able to pay fees." At this time Thomas would have been about 70 years old and Elizabeth had possibly already died. Mary Candis was probably an indentured servant belonging to Thomas.

More Money Matters (Back in Court Again)

June 1751 . . . Anne Arundel County Court Minutes. Thomas is back in court again, this time to answer charges of non-payment of a bill covering 20 pounds of sugar, 3 gallons and five pints of rum, a package of tea, and 3 pounds of lent (unable to identify), totaling five pounds five shillings due to William Hall of Elk Ridge (about 6 miles southwest of Baltimore on the Patapsco River). The matter was delayed until 10 March 1752, when the "the sheriff brought into court 12 good and lawful men of this bailiwick [a bailiff's or sheriff's jurisdiction] who being sworn to the truth said that Jackson [Jacks] did not assume upon himself in manner and form as the said William Hall above against him had complained." The said Hall recovered no monies, was required to pay court cost plus a fine for his "false clamour," and Thomas Jacks was free to go. Here Thomas would have been about 76 years old.

Death of Thomas Jacks Sr.

Thomas Jacks Sr. slipped from the pages of history almost as
quietly as he entered them. One source reports his death as 23
October 1756 and recorded in St. Paul Queen Church Parish.
Another source reports "a record of the administration of the
estate of Thomas Jacks, dated 20 January 1755, in Anne
Arundel County, Maryland, with administrators son Richard
Jacks, son in law Nicholas Peddicoat [husband of daughter
Anne] and Luke Mercier/Mercer [husband of daughter Barbara
or 'Barbary']." While there may be slight variances, we can be
relatively certain Thomas Jacks died around 1755 and was
buried in Anne Arundel County, Maryland. We know his children were living around him at the time of his death. His age
when he died would have been around eighty.

Some sources show his wife Elizabeth died around 1726 but
this is unlikely, as her name appears on the court records with
Thomas in the case of the orphaned Huit children. Here the
Elizabeth is specifically identified as his wife. That court event
took place in 1736 and was the last record found for Elizabeth,
so we may assume that Elizabeth died sometime after 1736. In
1736 Elizabeth would have been about 61 years old. She had
four children before she married Thomas, two by John Powell
and two by Christopher Walters. She and Thomas then had five
more. Assuming Elizabeth lived till at least 1736, she would
have seen Benjamin Franklin begin publishing the "Pennsylvania
Gazette", the city of Baltimore founded literally under her feet,
the birth of George Washington, both King George I and II
becoming kings of England, the English colony of Georgia
founded, and the first edition of Ben Franklin's Poor Richard's
Almanac. These two Jacks ancestors were a part in one of the
most exciting chapters of America's history.

CHAPTER 3

RICHARD JAMES JACKS

7 June 1713 – 16 October 1787
Anne Arundel County, Maryland

Life in the British Colonies

Richard James Jacks was born 7 June 1713 to Thomas Jacks Sr. and wife Elizabeth Gardner. Richard was born in Anne Arundel County in the Royal Colony of Maryland, near modern day Annapolis. That city was named for Princess Anne, younger sister of Queen Mary of England, who would later become Queen Anne. Annapolis is about 20 miles from Baltimore, named for Lord Baltimore. Annapolis was the social, political, and economic center of the colony. The area was originally settled by Puritans. Its rich soil was initially ideal for the growing of tobacco. Because tobacco farming was so labor intensive, it was heavily dependent on slave labor. Tobacco farming was also extremely hard on the soil, rapidly depleting its nutrients. By the time Richard was born in 1713, tobacco farmers like Richard's father Thomas Sr. were experiencing significant economic hardships. Yet, in spite of the economic downturn in the area's chief crop, population of the Annapolis and Baltimore area continued to grow. This area on the Chesapeake was one of the fastest growing areas in the colonies.

Richard was born in one of the principal population and economic hubs of the Chesapeake colonies. He was christened on 20 September 1713 at All Hallow Parish Church (Church of England which would become the Episcopal Church). In the Maryland area, this was by far the predominant denomination. However, as pre-revolutionary tensions grew between the colonies and England, the church came into great disfavor because of its largely Loyalist or Tory membership.

Land, a Wife, Spirits, and Children

About 1734 Richard married Ann Garland, the daughter of John Garland. She was born in Charles City County, Virginia, about 1715. Charles City County is near Richmond, in the heart of Virginia's tobacco growing region. Their marriage is believed to be recorded in St. Thomas Parish Church, near Baltimore, which is still an active church. It has been restored while leaving much of the original structure intact. It also has an old cemetery. St. Thomas Parish Church is approximately 30 miles from Annapolis. Richard was about 21 years old, Ann about nineteen at the time of their marriage. A year later, their first child, Elizabeth, was born. Elizabeth was probably named after Richard's mother. Two years later in 1737, their first son, Thomas, was born and most likely named after Richard's father.

It seems Richard had a taste for spirits. In 1738, when he was approximately 25 years old, the Anne Arundel County court records read as follows: "His Lordship: Richard Jacks and Phil Howard. The said Jacks having recorded with Phillip Howard his Security for his appearance at this court to answer plea, appears and confesses himself guilty of abusing a Magistrate and getting drunk and swearing whereupon the Court adjudges the said Jacks to pay the sum of 20 shillings for abusing a magistrate and 12 shillings 6 pence for being drunk and swearing which he pays to Sheriff, whereupon Tho Bishop becomes Security for the

fees due to the several officers of the court and he is
discharged." The fact that he had to appear with a guarantor,
and appears not to have enough cash to pay his fine – and has
another guarantor for the fine – may indicate Richard was not
one of the wealthy citizens of Anne Arundel County.

We know from the will of John Powell Jr., half-brother of
Richard Jacks, that Richard received a somewhat large parcel of
land from the Powell estate after the death of John Powell Jr.
This land was described in the will as "Powell's Inheritance on
South River." It is interesting how Richard got the land: John
Powel Jr. first willed the land to his mother Elizabeth during her
lifetime. After her death it was to pass to John Powell Jr.'s
younger brother Joseph and his heirs. This will was recorded on
6 April 1716. Elizabeth is believed to have died about 1726. To
that end on 15 August 1726, the younger brother of John
Powell, Joseph Powell, conveyed his inheritance of Powell's
Inheritance to his younger half-brother, Richard Jacks. Richard
was only 13 years old at the time. This property is described as
being on South River in Anne Arundel County. It was approximately 25 miles due east of the center of modern day Washington
D.C., and about five miles southwest of Annapolis. From a later
sale of land, we know Richard and Ann also had a 249-acre tract
of land located on "the north side of the main falls of the Patapsco
River" which flows through the present-day city of Baltimore and
into the Chesapeake Bay. This is a rather small river, and therefore
we can know that the property was no more than about 10 miles
due west of the Chesapeake Bay and Baltimore.

Their third child and second son, Richard Reuben, was born
about 1739, and John Nicholas Sr. the following year. Their fifth
child, William Martin, was born about 1742. Their last child to
be born in Anne Arundel County was Barbara about 1744. It
appears that sometime between 1744 and 1747 Richard and
Ann moved from Anne Arundel County to adjoining Baltimore

County. The move would have only been about 22 miles over well-developed roads.

Their seventh child, Nancy Ann, was born on 15 October 1747 in St. Thomas Parish, Baltimore County, Maryland. In 1748, their eight child, Rachel, was born. In July 1749 Richard and Ann purchased 40 acres, described as a part of "Fountain of Friendship," from George Turnbull, a carpenter and his wife Grace. Their last child, Edward, was born in September 1755. On 1 October 1762, another land purchase is recorded. They purchased 100 acres from William Wilson, a planter, and his wife Elizabeth for 53 pounds. It was described as the "south side of Morgans Run." This too was in Baltimore County. Somehow, even in the declining economic times of the 1760, Richard was making enough money to continue to purchase land.

The Family Leaves Maryland – Their Home for Almost 100 Years

Richard was born in Maryland, as was his father Thomas Sr. His grandfather had come from England in 1667 and made Maryland his home, too. For the past 98 years, Jone Jacks, Thomas Sr., and Richard had called Maryland home. But times were changing; Richard was a farmer or "planter" and he planted tobacco. The land was "wearing out." Year after year the tobacco crops had drained the nutrients from the soil. Crop rotation was either unheard of or unpracticed, and year after year crop yields and quality continued to fall. And yet, because of the vast plantations powered by large numbers of slaves, a tobacco surplus existed and market prices fell. The area where Richard lived, the Chesapeake, was known as "Tobacco Coast." The 1760s were a terrible time for tobacco planters. Richard's famous neighbor, George Washington, is reported to have lost 1,900 English pounds on his crop in 1760. While Washington's substantial family fortune enabled him to withstand the downturn, smaller farmers like Richard suffered significantly. This was happening on a large scale throughout the entire area.

At this same time, large tracts of land were becoming available in North Carolina. This new, unspoiled land, for sale at very reasonable prices proved a stronger force than the huge hardships associated with selling most of your family possessions, loading what you could into large carts pulled by oxen, and heading into a frontier wilderness. The area where Richard and Ann lived on the Chesapeake was a social, economic, and cultural center. The Yadkin Valley in North Carolina was the edge of the frontier.

On 29 October 1765, the Baltimore County Deed Records shows "Richard and Ann Jacks, planter, of Baltimore County Maryland to Robert Wier, farmer of same, for the sum of 300 pounds 249 acres north side of main falls of Patapsco River. Signed Richard Jacks. Wit: Nicholas Ruxton Gay and Samuel Owings." They had decided to make a significant life change. At the time of this sale, Richard was 52 and Ann was 50. They had been married over 30 years and now had nine children. Richard had probably never been more than fifty miles from his home until the move to North Carolina. They must have been excited and a bit nervous. But, to help keep things in perspective, Richard and Ann had help; daughter Elizabeth was 30 and not yet married. Son Thomas was 28, Richard was 26, John Nicholas was 25, and William was 23. Barbara was 21 and Nancy Ann was 18. Rachael was 17 and Richard was ten. All their children were still living at home, so there was plenty of help. We don't know exactly when they left Baltimore County. There is a period of almost three years where we have no record either in Maryland or in North Carolina.

The Yadkin Valley – New Home to the Jacks Clan

Richard and Ann and their large family arrived in the Yadkin

Valley sometime after the October 1765 property sale. Some family historians believe that son John Nicholas Sr. married Asenith Martin in 1767 in Rowan County, while others believe they married in 1769. If the earlier date is correct then the non-sourced date would close the missing time slightly. But by 7 September 1768 a deed is recorded in Rowan County which reads as follows: "Joseph Bryan and wife Alice sold to Richard Jacks for the sum of 65 pounds North Carolina money, 697 acres on both sides of Dutchman's Cedar and Cubb Creeks, adj. to Squire Boone and Isaac Tree. Witness: William Steel, John Jacks (son) and John Braly." Richard and Ann had two noteworthy neighbors; Squire Boone was Daniel's father, and John Lincoln who was the great-grandfather of President Abraham Lincoln. It's interesting to note that individual colonies were sometimes using their currency rather than the English pound.

By 8 February 1771, a deed is recorded selling part of this same tract of land (500 acres), to "John Brunts, shoemaker." Richard and Ann received 90 pounds for the tract of land. They had purchased the original 697 acres for only 65 pounds, so disregarding any inflation, they had made a profit on the sale, while retaining 197 acres. Later that same year, on 1 November 1771, Richard and Ann sell the remaining 197 acres to Abraham Adams for a sum of 40 pounds. By this time Richard was 58 and perhaps finding that 697 acres of land was a bit too much to maintain. Sons Richard and John Nicholas had already married; Richard lived just a few miles away in Surry County, and John Nicholas lived nearby in Rowan County. The household was slowly emptying.

In the meantime, the Yadkin Valley was "giving birth" to the Revolution. Oppression by the crown and its local agents, in the form of illegal taxation on virtually anything that could be taxed had pushed the residents of the Yadkin Valley into near revolt. The "War of the Regulation" took place here in the spring of

1771, and was one more nail in the coffin of the British Crown Colonies. Richard, Ann, and their children were living in the very area where American patriots would begin openly resisting the crown. Resentment of England ran high. The political situation had to dominate all aspects of life. Salisbury, the nearest town to Richard and Ann, was at the time the judicial center for the entire area. Therefore many of the issues against the crown went to court in the town where Richard and Ann bought their supplies.The Boston Non-Importation Agreement had been in effect for about two years and other parts of the colonies were starting to cut back on their trade with England. Shortages were becoming common.

In 1773 the Boston Tea Party occurred, and talk of open rebellion against the crown was everywhere. But the crown had its "loyalist" supporters as well. These Tories were numerous. Everybody had one or more as a neighbor. The mood in Rowan County was tense. About 1774 son Edward would marry Sarah Jones. In September of that same year, the first Continental Congress met. Most of Richard and Ann's neighbors believed armed conflict would be unavoidable. In October of 1774 the Articles of Association was passed. This was a universal prohibition of trade with England. What had been economic and principled abstinence was now a law. The last of anything imported from England disappeared from the store shelves. This placed an increased demand on the labors and ingenuity of the wives as they begin looking for ways to substitute local items for those household goods previously imported from England. To the aging Ann Jacks and her daughters and daughters-in-law these were indeed hard times.

In 1775 Patrick Henry made his famous "give me liberty or give me death" speech, Paul Revere made his ride, "the shot heard around the world" was fired at Lexington and Concord, the Second Continental Congress was held, George Washington was named Commander in Chief, the Battle of Bunker Hill took place, and Jacks sons Thomas, Richard, and John Nicholas joined the North Carolina Militia. The Revolutionary War suddenly became very real to the family of Richard and Ann Jacks.

In 1779 daughter Rachel married Samuel Thomas Bryant in Rowan County. The British intensified their attacks in the southern colonies, as fighting raged all through Georgia and the Carolinas. Rowan County Militia patriots were in numerous conflicts. Both patriot and loyalist Tory troops, hungry and in desperate need of supplies foraged through the countryside, taking by force what would not be freely supplied. If it had value and could walk or be moved, it was taken. Food was in critical supply; those in the countryside who were accustomed to hunting and fishing fared better than those living in Salisbury. Still, many of the men were away often with the militia and those tasks normally done by the men fell to the women. By 1779, Richard was 66 years old, and as far as we know, age kept him out of the war. He would have been of some assistance in trying to help the family survive.

On 15 March 1781, in Greensboro – less than 50 miles from their home – the famous Battle of Guilford Courthouse took place. Since a significant number of the patriot troops were North Carolina militia, it is highly probable that sons Thomas, Richard, and John were in the battle. While the patriots officially lost the 90-minute battle, the British lost over one quarter of their troops. It ranks as one of the war's most decisive battles, in marking a turning point in the war. British control of Georgia and South Carolina – which had also been hoped to extend to North Carolina – began to come unraveled at the battle of Guilford Courthouse. While Thomas, Richard, and John were probably in the battle, they were certainly fighting against their neighbors as many local Tories had joined with the British troops. However, the longer the war raged on, the more that the British began to have problems finding eager supporters among the loyalist Tories. It was becoming clear to many Tories that they had chosen the wrong side.

By mid-1782 it was also becoming increasingly clear to the British that they were losing the war and the cost to continue was higher than they were willing to pay. They began withdrawing their troops from Georgia and the Carolinas. A political crisis in Britain was taking place. By November the British and Americans had signed preliminary articles of peace. By April of 1783 the Continental Congress had ratified the agreement, and in September of that year the British and Americans signed the Treaty of Paris. The war was officially over, but the patriot troops did not come home to victory celebrations. They returned to face financial ruin as their farms lay neglected and gutted by foraging militias and looters. The economy was in shambles; recovery would be slow and painful.

Five years later, in failing health at the age of 74, Richard James Jacks made out his will. Not only is it interesting to get a glimpse into his thoughts, but perhaps even more interesting, here in his will, we see the style and morality of a Revolutionary War-era last will and testament. The will of Richard James Jacks is recorded in the Rowan County North Carolina Will Book C, page 69, dated 16 October 1787 and reads as follows:

"In the name of God, amen. I, Richard Jacks of Rowan County, State of North Carolina, being sick and weak of body and perfect mind and memory, thanks be given to God for it, calling to mind the mortality of my body and that it is appointed for all men once to die. Do make and ordain this to be my last will and testament. Principally and first of all I give and recommend my soul into the hands of God that gave it to me and my body I recommend to the earth to be buried in a decent Christian like manner at the discretion of my executors, nothing doubting but the General Resurrection, I shall receive the same again by the mighty power of God and as touching such worldly goods as it hath pleased God to bless me with, I give and dispose in manner and form as followeth:

Item: I will and declare that the tract of land that I now live on be the property of my beloved wife Ann during her life and also the one half of all my stock with one half of my household furniture and after death I will and bequeath said land, stock, and household furniture to my daughter Elizabeth Jacks. I will and bequeath to my daughter Elizabeth the other half of my stock and the other half of my household furniture to her and her heirs forever. I will and bequeath unto my son Thomas, the sum of five shillings lawful money to be paid out of my estate by my executors and no more. I will and bequeath unto my son Richard five shillings lawful money to be paid out of my estate by my executors and no more. I will and bequeath unto my son John Jacks five shillings lawful money to be paid out of my estate and no more. I will and bequeath to my son William Jacks five shillings lawful money to be paid out of my estate by my executors and no more. I give and bequeath to my daughters Barbara and Ann the sum of five shillings to each lawful money to be paid out of my estate by my executors and no more. I will and bequeath to my daughter Rachel, the sum of five shillings to be paid out of my estate by my executors and no more.

Item: I constitute and appoint my beloved wife Ann and my beloved son John my sole executors of this my last will and testament. In witness whereof I have hereto set my hand and seal this 16th day of October 1787. Signed, sealed, and published and pronounced in the presence of: Hardy Jones, Isaac Enochs and Michael Beard. Richard Jacks {seal}

On the following day, 17 October 1787, Richard James Jacks died. He was buried on his own property, known as Hanging Rock, just south of the Yadkin River. It is believed that his wife Ann lived with daughter Elizabeth, wife of William Snow, after Richard's death. By this time Elizabeth, their oldest child, was 52.

About 1800, Ann Garland Jacks died, at the age of about 85. She was buried beside Richard on their property. According to Richard's will, Hanging Rock passed to Ann, and at Ann's death, Hanging Rock went to daughter Elizabeth Jacks Snow. In 1803 she sold the property. The following deed was recorded in Rowan County North Carolina Land Deed Book 19, page 1: "William Snow and wife Elizabeth to Philip Haynes, 163 acres of land exception 33 feet where Richard and Ann Jacks are buried."

The life story of Richard and Ann reads like a novel. They were born in the beginning of the 1700s in colonial America and raised in the heart of America's tobacco growing region. They were contemporaries of Washington, Jefferson, Franklin, Thomas Paine, and Paul Revere. They moved from the comfortable life of the Chesapeake Bay to the edge of America's frontier, the Yadkin Valley, where their neighbor was Squire Boone, the father of Daniel Boone. They watched the drama of the American Revolution unfold, and had three sons serve in the Revolutionary War. Without the benefit of modern medicine, they survived epidemics and infections. They had nine children who reached adulthood. Their marriage lasted 53 years and it was only death that parted them.

CHAPTER 4

JOHN NICHOLAS JACKS SR.

About 1740 – About 1830
Anne Arundel County, Maryland

The Colonial America of John's Early Years

About 1740, just outside today's Annapolis, Maryland, near
Baltimore, John Nicholas Jacks Sr., fourth child and third son of
Richard James Jacks and Ann Garland, was born. John's parents
belonged to the Church of England, or Anglican Church, known
today as the Protestant Episcopal Church. The area where John
was born was a prosperous center of trade. Shipbuilding, sail
making, oyster packing, all contributed greatly to the area's
economy. John lived in the heart of colonial America; for a time,
after the Treaty of Paris in 1783, Annapolis would become the
temporary capitol of the newly independent colonies. It was also
there that General George Washington would resign his commis-
sion as commander-in-chief of the victorious Colonial Army and
return to civilian life. Washington's home, Mount Vernon, was
only thirty miles away. These were exciting but unstable times.

Judging from the large tract of land that John's father
Richard owned, Richard appears to have been a planter. We
have found no evidence that they were members of Maryland's
inner social circles. John lived in a time and an area that had

many extremely well educated men, including the most illustrious years of Benjamin Franklin. He was three when Thomas Jefferson was born, and Thomas Paine was three years old when John Jacks was born. Yet, from an obscure footnote in history – a land transaction recorded in a Rowan County, North Carolina, land deed book on 27 October 1783 – we see where John Jacks signed with an "X". John would grow up to be illiterate.

In light of John's lack of education, it's doubtful that his family dressed in the aristocratic style of the Washington, Jefferson, and Adams families. Therefore when he went to social gatherings, he probably didn't see many ladies and gentlemen wearing wigs and fine clothes considered so essential to the gentry of the day. The colonial America of John's day was still very much rooted in the class system which dominated England. If you were born in a class, you stayed in that class. Obviously, opportunities existed in America for those with entrepreneurial spirit, opportunities unavailable to those across the ocean in England. Such opportunities made it possible for immigrants to come penniless to America from Europe as indentured servants and succeed. Indeed, John's great-grandfather Jone Jacks had done exactly that. But this was a possibility and not a guarantee.

In the Chesapeake Bay area where John grew up, tobacco dominated every aspect of life. It was the cash crop of the colony – and was even used as cash. Tobacco had been the economic bastion of the Chesapeake area since the time of the first settlers. But tobacco plants depleted the soil's natural nutrients, and soon much land was incapable of producing even minimal crops of food or tobacco. In addition, the price of tobacco was unstable; bringing the product to market involved numerous levels of middlemen. The plight of the average tobacco grower became dire. Many were losing their land to creditors. The merchants, who did not risk their land or toil on it, were reaping all the profits, while the small and medium-size farmers were facing ruin. Many were getting out of the business or moving on to new frontiers with cheaper land and soil that was not depleted. Many of John's neighbors were selling their land if they could, taking their slaves, and moving to frontier areas where land was fertile and cheap. One of these new frontiers was North Carolina. This was the atmosphere surrounding young John Sr., as he was growing into manhood.

We cannot be sure that John's father Richard was caught up in all this. Richard had been acquiring land in the Chesapeake area regularly through October 1762. But by 29 October 1765, John's father Richard and his wife Ann started selling their land in the Baltimore area and began their move to the Yadkin Valley in Rowan County North Carolina. Twenty-eight-year-old bachelor John moved with them.

The Jacks Family Migrates to North Carolina – Farewell to Maryland, their Home from 1668 – 1768

Since all Richard and Ann's children married while in North Carolina, it is assumed all nine of their children accompanied them to Rowan County. John's family arrived along with thousands of others in one of America's most significant migration events. Years earlier, Britain's King Charles II had given large tracts of land to certain influential British subjects, and later, King George II did the same. In the early 1760s this land – which had for the most part remained vacant – began being sold off to the public at very attractive prices. This, combined with lands damaged by decades of tobacco farming in Maryland, fueled a truly spectacular migration to North Carolina. In 1766, Governor Tryon is reported to have said he believed North Carolina was being settled faster than any other province. New settlements in Rowan County were being created almost daily. We believed John's family settled somewhere between Salisbury and the Yadkin River. The land along the rivers in this area was extremely fertile. Land records showed their property lay along the North Fork of the Yadkin River, very likely within ten miles of present-day Salisbury.

The trip was just over 300 miles. The roads were bad by the standards of today. By the time John and all his relatives made the journey, around 1768, the "wagon road" was in place. The wagon road's beginnings lay in winding Indian foot trails, which later morphed into wider paths, suitable for packsaddle trains. Such trails were three to four feet wide. Finally, the roads had been worn wide enough to accommodate large carts and wagons. Still, ten miles a day would be considered a good day and five-mile days were not uncommon, especially when the roads were muddy or the wagon required repair. It was almost certain John and his family came in these large wagons. Most nights would have been spent out in the open. The common practice was to stop beside the road about mid-afternoon in order to make camp and feed the animals before dark. Thieves, both Indian and outlaws, were still a problem so travelers would camp in groups for protection. Disease and death were no strangers to those who were part of this great migration toward new frontier lands. When John's family traveled this road, some believe it was the most heavily traveled road in the colonies. Governor Tryon wrote to England that more than a thousand wagons passed through Salisbury in the fall and winter of 1765, which works out to about six immigrant wagons per day. The Jacks family arrived in the Salisbury area in the midst of this explosive growth.

What They Found – Pre-Revolutionary Yadkin Valley

Early surveyor reports described the Yadkin Valley as a paradise. The Indians were friendly, the soil was incredibly fertile, and wildlife of all types abounded. Timber and stones were abundant for building, and the land was relatively easy to clear.

Records indicate John owned close to 2000 acres of this magnificent frontier land. We don't know exactly how long John lived with his father and mother after they arrived in the valley but it was not long. At the time the family arrived, John was already 28 years old. While no record of his marriage can be found, we know he married eighteen-year-old Asenith Martin, daughter of John Martin, about 1767. This rather unusual name comes from the Bible. In the book of Genesis, Pharaoh gave the daughter of Potipherah, a high-ranking Egyptian priest of On, to Joseph for a wife. Asenith (or Asenath) bore Joseph two sons, Manasseh and Ephraim. They of course became the patriarchs of the two Israelite tribes Manasseh and Ephraim.

Another possible scenario about when and how the Jacks family came to the Yadkin Valley, for which there is circumstantial support, is that John came to North Carolina prior to the family's final property sell-offs back in Anne Arundel County, Maryland. Since this was a wilderness John could have come with his father on an exploratory and property-buying trip. We see John's father Richard starting to liquidate and sell his properties back in Anne Arundel County as early as 1765. But it was not until three years later, in 1768, that we find the first property purchase recorded in Rowan County by Richard. John's marriage year to Asenith is believed to be 1767, a year prior to the first property purchase by his father. John had two older brothers who also settled in the Yadkin Valley; Thomas, born about 1737, and Richard, born about 1739. Both Richard and Thomas later owned land adjoining John and Asenith's. John and one or more of his older brothers could have been in the area prior to 1768. But by 1769 John is shown on the Rowan County tax roll as having paid one poll tax.

By 1775 John and Asenith had land surveyed on the south side of the Yadkin River which adjoined his brother Richard's property. For whatever reason, this 640-acre land purchase was not recorded until 18 June 1778. At the same time, two other tracts of land were recorded for John and Asenith, each for 500 acres. Because of the size of these holdings it is highly improbable he was able to cultivate all this land; therefore the possibility exists that John and Asenith were speculating with some of their land-holdings.

The Revolutionary War – John Jacks, Private, Artillery, North Carolina Militia

The delay of the recording or perhaps the finalization of the purchase referenced above could have been due to the insecurity of the times. In 1775 fears and rumors of war abounded. It is hard to imagine living in such instability. On 23 March 1775, Patrick Henry gave his famous "Give me liberty or give me death" speech. On 18 April, Paul Revere made his ride. A day later the Minutemen and the Redcoats clashed at Lexington and Concord and the shot was heard around the world. On 10 May, the Second Continental Congress met in Philadelphia. On 17 June, the Battle of Bunker Hill took place. George Washington took command of the Continental Armies on 3 July. Virginia and North Carolina patriots drove out the Loyalists troops and burned Norfolk on 11 December. While the Declaration of Independence was not signed until 1776, in reality, the colonies were already at war. If events of this magnitude took place today, stock and commodity markets around the world would convulse. The diverse local economies of the colonies – already in turmoil – must have come to a near standstill. John and Asenith would, by 1775, already have three children; John Nicholas Jr., Richard Marion, and Thomas.

We don't know if John Nicholas Jacks Sr. was an enthusiastic patriot who couldn't wait to join the fight against the British and their loyalist Tory supporters. We don't know if he joined the fight due to social pressure, or perhaps it was out of necessity to protect his home, his family, his livestock, and his property. The situation found John as a private in the artillery division of North Carolina's Militia; one way or the other, staying out of the fight was not an option. The Rowan County Militia fought bravely in numerous battles and skirmishes. Many were killed and many were taken prisoner. All suffered significant property loss. If something was alive and could be eaten or ridden or used to pull or carry something, it was taken, either by the Tories or by hungry and under-equipped patriot forces. We have specific evidence this unauthorized taking of property by militias or armies touched John and Asenith. In 1782, John was one of the several signers of a "Remonstrance & Petition From Inhabitants of Salisbury District." These petitioners were seeking compensation for their movable property which had been unlawfully taken during the fighting.

Life in Rowan County during the Revolutionary War was horrible for both the "loyalists" Tories and the patriots. Today, unless we've studied this era carefully, it's easy to visualize John's environment as the brave colonists fighting the British. But in reality, it was far from that. In many aspects, it resembled a civil war. In some cases neighbor was fighting neighbor. And these battles were bloody. The militias were under-equipped and under-fed. While John was in his late thirties, many combatants were merely teenagers. Soldiers, civilians, Indians – they were all combatants. Death, hunger, and the destruction of property were everywhere. With each day the situation became more desperate.

In the early stages of the fighting, John was able to join up with the other militiamen, go fight a battle, then return home and care for his family and crops. This was one benefit of being in a militia. But as the fighting dragged on year after year, things changed; conditions back on their farms and with their families had worsened to the point it was hard to think of anything else.

When John and his compatriots first signed up with the militia, it was possible to visualize peace through some type of settlement which would allow things to return to normal. But by 1780 the average militiaman had come to view the only way out as death or victory. Sometimes in fiercely fought battles, hundreds would fall. Only poor attempts could be made to bury the dead, and as often as not they were left unburied. Sometimes the families of the dead would come to the scene of the battle to claim the bodies of their loved ones. This was not the war seen in paintings depicting some courageous general on horseback, leading the charge. This was carnage of the highest degree. This was the life of John Nicholas Jacks Sr. during his military service.

Asenith's life while John was gone similarly became more difficult. For years, in response to the British imposition of unjust taxes, the colonists had embargoed many British goods. They had to learn to either do without these goods or make some kind of substitute from the resources they had available. These hardships fell mostly on the wives in the colonies and Asenith was certainly no exception. But John managed to spend time away from the battles. This was evidenced by the birth of their first daughter, Mary "Polly" Jacks, who was born about 1778. There was a child born in 1781 and another in 1783, both of whom apparently died in infancy.

Finally, with British General Cornwallis's surrender at Yorktown, Virginia, on 19 October 1781, peace would slowly begin to return to the colonies. The Revolutionary War was formally ended by the Treaty of Paris is 1783. For the victorious patriots, considering the damage to property, the economy, and the loss of family members, victory could hardly be called sweet. It just offered an end to the suffering and a hope for a return to normality sometime in the future. All knew that time was a long way off, and perhaps for some, it would never come. Thousands upon thousands of the loyalists left for England or Canada. The face of the Yadkin Valley would never be the same.

The Jacks Family in Salisbury – Another Famous Neighbor

In 1785 Anna Jacks was born. Land transactions for John and Asenith were also recorded during this period. They purchased 204 acres in Salisbury, adjoining Asa Martin, Asenith's brother. This could have been another land investment. All their property was in the close vicinity of Salisbury and in the general Yadkin Valley area of Rowan County. It was also about this time, in 1789, fourth son William Milton was born. From later recorded documents, we learn that for all practical purposes, John and Asenith were residents of Salisbury.

In 1784 a young man of questionable success thus far in life moved to Salisbury and apprenticed in a law office there; his name – Andrew Jackson. Salisbury was a small town at that time, and John and Asenith had lived in the Salisbury area since 1769. John had numerous land transactions, served on a grand jury, and was part of what would today be called a class-action lawsuit petitioning for damages suffered to his property during the Revolution. It's almost certain he would have known the young law clerk and later, by about 1787, attorney Andrew Jackson. In 1787, John's father Richard's will was filed in Salisbury. Young Andrew Jackson would have received his law license that year.

The Call of Kentucky

As the fighting came to an end, families could begin to rebuild their shattered lives. Many of North Carolina's residents had been killed. There was not yet much stabilizing influence from any kind of federal government. The economy was in shambles; the new federal government was deep in debt as were

the states. Agricultural prices fell as the war demand ceased.
They no longer had a favored status in Britain for their products.
The British made sure they were excluded from their previous
markets in the British West Indies. Unemployment soared in the
cities. Times were anything but good.

The government had already learned that by opening new
lands for settlement the economy would be stimulated. They
began to do this. During the war, much of the frontier was not a
safe place for civilians. The British had organized and armed
many Indian tribes and encouraged them to attack the settlers
who were streaming into the Indian's hunting grounds. Many
Indian tribes were only too happy to oblige the British. The
tactic was to a large degree successful; keeping significant
numbers of the colonists busy defending themselves against
Indian attacks and out of the eastern conflicts. The British were
then able to focus their war efforts on the American seaports
and large cities of the northeast – all this being done with Indian
combatants rather than the hard-pressed British regular troops.
Many early settlers decided these Indian dangers increased the
risks of living on the new frontier to a point past what they were
willing to endure. But with the Treaty of Paris in 1783, the war
officially ended. What would soon become the state of Kentucky
was at the time, Kentucky County, Virginia. Its residents were
eager for statehood. Efforts toward that goal began in earnest in
1784 shortly after the Treaty of Paris, as settlers began streaming
into Kentucky.

Some years earlier, in September of 1773, just before serious
fighting began in the Yadkin Valley, the Jacks family had
watched their neighbor Daniel Boone pack up and leave for
Kentucky. He led a group of about fifty emigrants from the
Yadkin Valley and surrounding areas to the new frontier, but his
timing was not right. A few days after Boone and his family
arrived in the Kentucky frontier area, his oldest son, James,

along with some other men and boys, were captured and tortured to death by a band of Indians. They abandoned their settlement effort soon afterwards, but in 1775 Boone returned and established a small frontier community and fort called Boonesborough.

John Jacks and his family were no doubt following Boone's activities as well as the progress toward statehood. We don't know how long they had been planning to follow Boone and others from North Carolina to Kentucky, but it is certain this was their plan. On 2 November 1790, we see where John served as a member of the Rowan County grand jury. But later that month John and Asenith began to sell off their holdings in North Carolina. On 20 November 1790 a sale is recorded. By this time, a large population migration from North Carolina into Kentucky was already underway.

Not all in the Jacks family were focused on the move to Kentucky. Sometime in 1790, possibly in anticipation of this move and not wanting to leave behind the 19-year-old love of his life, first son, 20-year-old John Nicholas Jr., married Sarah Keen. When his parents made their move to Kentucky, John Jr., and his bride Sarah would stay behind for a while.

On 1 January 1791 more land sales are recorded for John and Asenith. On 12 February of the same year they sold even more land. We don't know exactly when they made their actual move to Kentucky but it was probably close to this time. Kentucky ratified its state constitution in 1792 and on 1 June of that same year became a state; the Commonwealth of Kentucky, the first state admitted west of the Appalachians. "Kentucky fever" was running high in Rowan County.

Some sources show daughter Mary "Polly" and Nathaniel Wilson married in Montgomery County, Kentucky, about 1794, but records for that period were reported destroyed by a fire in 1851 and a later fire during the Civil War. If true, this would

establish John and Asenith in Kentucky by 1794. The marriage
of their second son, Richard Marion, to Sophia Barnes is
recorded on 23 February 1797, in Madison County, Kentucky.
This was near Fort Boonesborough where neighbor Daniel
Boone brought his family when they first came to the area. By
the time the Jacks family arrived Daniel had moved on and Fort
Boonesborough had been abandoned due to Indian attacks
shortly after being founded.

John and Asenith's son John Jr. and his wife Sarah ("Sally")
had not yet joined them in Kentucky. They remained back in
Rowan County for a while, as evidenced by the recorded birth
of Thomas in 1791, Penelope in 1793, James Keen in 1795, and
Lucy in 1796. But John Jr.'s fifth child, son John Greenberry, was
born in 1798 in Montgomery County, Kentucky. As they had in
the past and would in the future, they stayed together, at least
for a while. We believe John Jr. did not stay in this area as long
as John Sr.'s other children. They would depart the Lexington
area around 1806 and move south to Gallatin County, Kentucky.

John Nicholas Sr. appears on the Montgomery County,
Kentucky, tax list on 22 August 1800. The United States Census
for 1810 lists John, Asenith, and two females ages between 16
and 26 living in Bourbon County. These two females were probably daughters Anna, born 1785 and married in Bath County in
1822, and Tabitha, born about 1794 and married in Bath
County in 1816. By the time of this census John would have
been 70 years old, and his wife Asenith, about 59.

Sometime after the 1810 census and before the census of
1820, John's wife Asenith died. We do not have the exact date,
but it is believed she died in Bourbon County around 1818. She
would have been nearly 70 years old and married to John
almost 50 years. She must have been a strong woman, both
emotionally and physically. She endured life on the frontier–a
life with no modern medicines, a life where medical practices

still included "blood-letting." She gave birth to at least ten children. She held the family and farm together while John was off with the militia fighting the Revolutionary War. She was a part in two major population migrations toward new frontiers; Maryland to North Carolina, and then North Carolina to Kentucky. Asenith Martin Jacks was a grand matriarch of our Jacks family.

The 1810 census also shows John and Asenith's son Richard and his family living nearby in Madison County. In Richard's household was Richard's younger brother William Milton and his wife Nancy White. At this time Richard would have been about 38 years old and his younger brother William 21 years old. By the 1820 United States Census, John was widowed. Only daughter Anna remained unmarried. John would have been 80 years old at this time and Anna near 35. John was living with son Thomas and it also appears Anna was living with Thomas. Anna would marry John Layton two years later. In true Jacks fashion, John is surrounded by family. The 1820 census also shows neighbors of Thomas to be his brothers-in-law Nathaniel Wilson, husband of John's daughter Mary "Polly," and William White, husband of John's daughter Tabitha.

While we see Madison, Montgomery, Bath, and Bourbon counties in their residences, if held in prospective they are all within 30 miles of Lexington, Kentucky. The city of Lexington was founded in 1782 – although occupied by frontiersmen as early as 1775, when still a part of Virginia. By the time the Jacks family arrived in the area about fifteen years later, Lexington was a booming town, famous for wealth and sophistication in the heart of Kentucky's fertile Bluegrass Region.

We don't have a lot of information about John Nicholas Jacks Sr.'s last years. He is believed to have died between 1826 and 1830, while living with his third son Thomas. He would have been about 86 to 90 years old. He led a truly amazing life;

a contemporary and neighbor to Daniel Boone, participating in two historic American population migrations, and a contemporary and neighbor of Andrew Jackson. He fought in the American Revolution as part of the North Carolina militia. He lived at the same time as Washington, Jefferson, Hamilton, Franklin, Napoleon, and Beethoven. He saw the Declaration of Independence written, as well as the Constitution of the United States and the Bill of Rights. He lived during the French Revolution, the execution of King Louis XVI of France and Marie Antoinette. He survived the horrors of the American Revolution as well as an entire lifetime on the American frontier. He died, full of years, surrounded by his children, and grand-children, and probably great-grand-children.

CHAPTER 5

JOHN NICHOLAS JACKS JR.

About 1770 – About 1851
Rowan County, North Carolina

A Pre-Revolution Frontier America Childhood

John Nicholas Jacks Jr., the first child of John Nicholas Jacks and Asenith Martin, was born about 1770 in Yadkin Valley, Rowan County, North Carolina. He was born on "British Soil" . . . in a colony belonging to Great Britain. John was six years old when the colonists signed the Declaration of Independence.

Yadkin Valley – Life on The Frontier

In 1770, the approximate year of John Nicholas Jacks Jr.'s birth, the Yadkin Valley was a breathtakingly beautiful area populated by large landowners. The Jacks family was one of those large landowning families. Richard Jacks, John's grandfather, brought his family, including John Nicholas's father John Nicholas Sr., to the Yadkin Valley in 1765. They came there from the Anne Arundel area of Maryland, near Baltimore. They were part of a large migration into the Yadkin Valley area which began around 1752, but had slowed considerably for a while due to increased hostilities by the Cherokee. These hostilities were to a large part a result of agitation and encouragement by the French, eventually leading to the French and Indian War in 1754. After the war, immigration once again resumed and Richard Jacks was a part of this migration wave. The people coming to the region during this time were basically not new immigrants to America but second and third generation colonists, mostly from England. This was the case with John's family.

While the Indian problems were settled for the moment, the issue of corruption within the provincial government and local levels was worsening at an alarming rate. The government officials, for the most part, had no salaries from England and had to "generate" their salaries from taxation. This resulted in intolerable abuses, and in some cases citizens had their land seized and sold for nonpayment of these taxes. Often there was no currency with which to pay the tax. The situation escalated to the point of violence; aside from being beautiful and blessed with resources, the valley had its darker side as well. This was the Yadkin Valley of John Jr.'s childhood.

Their Neighbor – Squire Boone: Father of Daniel Boone

The Jacks family land adjoined the land of Daniel Boone's father and well-known pioneer Squire Boone. It's very probable that John Jr. knew Daniel Boone personally. Because so much has been written about their famous neighbor, we are able to know about life in the Yadkin Valley during John's childhood.

This was a land of exceptional natural beauty, abounding with wild game of all types. People farmed, raised animals, planted fruit orchards, and fished the bountiful streams and rivers. The forests provided timber as well as their two primary wild game-meats, deer and bear. In addition, the deer hides were valuable as an export to England. The thick forests were cleared one tree at a time. The large landowners generally did not clear all the forest at once. They would plant corn around the tree stumps as there was no practical way to remove the stumps. It does not appear they used any organized form of crop rotation. Still, the land would produce adequate quantities of corn to feed both the settlers and their animals. They usually managed to find enough "extra" corn for distilling a bit of whiskey also. Corn and other vegetables were planted close to the house, where dogs could help scare away the deer.

In addition, the forest gave them maple syrup which was used as their primary sweetener. They managed to find a little "extra" maple syrup to distill into spirits also. "Sugaring", as the process of harvesting and making the sugar was called, involved boiling the maple sap down into syrup, or further down into granulated sugar. This took place in the last part of winter as the snow began to melt and the sap began to rise. There wasn't a lot of work involved, which also made the process popular. A tap would be driven in the maple tree and a container placed under the tap to catch the sap. "Sugaring parties" or groups would often go out into the woods where the maple trees were plentiful and build little camps where the process would take place. This was done to avoid the difficulty of transporting hundreds of gallons of heavy sap back home. Modern-day agricultural experts report one tap hole usually produces from five to fifteen gallons of sap, and about ten gallons of sap will produce about one quart of syrup. It was common to have no more than three taps per tree and usually only one or two. The parties would often build little huts or crude cabins in the vicinity of the maple trees where they could shelter from the cold weather and process the sap. The term "sugar shack" is believed to have come from this. The entire process was more or less regarded as a festive occasion.

Although no longer plentiful in the area, there were still some buffalo. Beaver abounded in the rivers and streams. They were trapped during the winter when their fur was the thickest. Their pelts were a good source of supplemental income. With the Indian threat no longer a problem in the valley, it's hard to imagine a more wonderful place for John Jr. to grow up . . . if the corruption were disregarded.

War and Rumors of War—The Colonies Struggle for Independence, 1774—1784

By the time John was four, the men talked of little else but the situation with the British. Some of their neighbors, referred to as Tories, favored keeping the status quo and working patiently with the British to improve the situation. However, the vast majority of the Jacks family's neighbors, while not outright favoring a war with England, saw few other options. It seemed a war was the only acceptable way for the colonies to go. Everyone was anxious. But by no means were the British the only problem facing the people of the Yadkin Valley. There was widespread civil unrest in all the colonies at this time. This unrest reached from Canada to South Carolina. There was little centrally-organized government which could benefit the common people. What government did exist basically was used by the wealthy class to enrich themselves and oppress everyone else. Corruption was unrestrained. Courts were quick to take homes and land for settlement of debts, and debtor's prison was frequently an option. The beautiful Yadkin Valley was full of very angry people.

The situation was complex. The United States in which John would someday live did not exist. There were only thirteen individual colonies, all with individual identities and self-interests, who, having formed provincial governments, agreed to band together and oppose the British. This opposition was basically over the heavy taxation Britain was levying on the colonies without giving them any say in the running of their affairs, either commercial or civil. Generations of living in America, surviving the harsh frontier life without any support or protection from England, had shaped the colonists into a strong and fiercely independent people. They would band together, at least temporarily, to resist and change the situation. For the people of North Carolina "the enemy" was not exclusively "the crown." Neighbors were enemies. The "loyalists" supported Britain and quickly joined local militias in support of the crown. Those who opposed likewise joined militias. The two sides skirmished regularly. Lives were lost, property destroyed, and a deep polarization of North Carolina's inhabitants set in.

Britain would not sit quietly as the colonists took these actions, and soon British combat troops began pouring into the colonies. By the spring of 1775, bullets were flying in the northern parts of the country. The war was no longer a possibility . . . it was a reality. Everywhere militias were forming. The Yadkin Valley would be pulled into the conflict. By the summer of 1776, the united colonies had issued a Declaration of Independence from Britain. The militia ranks would immediately swell.

John's family lived in an area of the colony which favored independence from Britain but the sentiment was not unanimous. Some in the colony still had strong business ties with England and feared the disruption to their livelihood a war would bring. They were nevertheless a very independent people who had to constantly fight local government taxation and corruption. They were for the most part people who lived close to the land. Soon after the War of Independence began, those favoring separation from England greatly outnumbered the "Loyalists" or Tories. The British army would soon call Rowan County "The Hornet's Nest" due to the extreme resistance they encountered from these freedom loving, independent citizens of the area. The feelings ran high and often mobs and vigilante groups moved unrestrained.

Young John Nicholas, in addition to growing up in the Yadkin Valley, also grew up in the midst of militia groups who were devoted to driving the British army out of North Carolina and along with them . . . their Tory sympathizers.

About a year after the signing of the Declaration of Independence, the North Carolina Revolutionary Government required all men of military age to sign an allegiance to the new government and to serve in one of North Carolina's many militias. With the exception of a few religious groups considered pacifists, military service was compulsory for all men of military age. The militias were full of teenagers. Serving on one of these militias was not necessarily like serving in the military. These men were all neighbors and while they had officers, most of their companies were loosely structured and more resembled a group of neighbors defending themselves than a highly disciplined military unit. This did not mean they were an ineffective fighting force; it just meant they were not like the British army or the Continental Army of General George Washington.

What had been a beautiful and peaceful valley was becoming a place of violence. To a boy approaching adolescence, this violence was probably a driving factor influencing and molding the character which would become evident as John Jr. grew to manhood. The carnage of this war was very real. Homes were commonly burned. Everything that could be eaten or used was carried off by the British army or by either the Tory militias or the militias of the patriots. With livestock and grain in critically short supply, prices began to rise. The general population believed that wealthy merchants (often Tories) were hoarding and manipulating the market, thus causing the price increases in order to profit from the hard times. Property that could not be carried away was often burned or otherwise destroyed in acts of retaliation. As the populations fled the fighting, nothing living was left behind. Before the end of the war, the area would be decimated. It would take years to recover from the damage of the war. In many cases, neighbor was fighting neighbor, and even the local Indian tribes were drawn into the fighting, some for the Tories and British, while some tribes joined with the revolutionaries. John Nicholas Jacks Jr. could not possibly have escaped being forever shaped by these experiences. It's difficult to know for sure, but all the destruction of property and livestock during the war could have played a part in the many Yadkin Valley residents leaving after the war. Many, like John Sr. and John Jr. plus other family members, later left the Yadkin Valley and migrated to Kentucky.

John Was A Baptist

At some point in his childhood, John Jr. was introduced to the Baptist faith. We have no direct information about this but his religious beliefs would prove a dominant influence throughout his life. From our research on early Baptist churches in North Carolina we are able to understand what John Jr.'s fundamental religious precepts were. The Baptist denomination to which he would later belong, began founding churches with great zeal in North Carolina around 1755. A key leader in this North Carolina Baptist movement was a man named Shubael Stearns. Stearns was reportedly greatly influenced by the famous minister Jonathan Edwards who was credited as being the moving force behind the rapid growth of the Baptist denomination in America, a period of rapid growth known as the Great Awakening. By the time John Jr. was born, around 1770, the denomination was thriving. The Baptists in the northern colonies referred to the Shubael Stearns Baptists as Separate Baptists due to the already growing rift between the northern and southern groups over the issue of slavery. The Separate Baptists would go on to eventually become what is referred to today as Southern Baptists. By the time John Jr. was a teenager the Separates were forming small groups known as missionary societies dedicated to spreading their faith on the edges of the frontier. The evidence is strong, though not confirmed, that John Jr. would later be active in one or more of these missionary society groups.

John Nicholas Jacks Jr. Takes a Wife

To date, no record of John's marriage to Sarah "Sally" Keen as been found, but predicated on the birth years of their children, it would have happened around 1790. Young John would have been about twenty years old. Family tradition says they were married in Timber Ridge, Rowan County, North Carolina. Sarah was the daughter of Nicholas Keen and Penelope Trammell, and was born about 1770 in Fairfax County, Virginia. The 1790 United States Census shows Nicholas Keen's family in Rowan County, North Carolina. Sarah was believed to be a Methodist but became a Baptist after her marriage to John Jr.

A Marriage of Almost Sixty Years – Twelve Children and Five States

John Jr. and Sarah "Sally" started their family almost immediately. For nearly sixty years they would hold this family together as it moved across North Carolina, Kentucky, Tennessee, Alabama, back to Tennessee, then finally to Mississippi. Their first child, son Thomas Jacks (probably named for John Jr.'s great-grandfather Thomas Jacks Sr.) , was born around 1791 in Rowan County. Their second child, a daughter named Penelope (probably named for Sally's mother Penelope Trammell Keen), was born 1 November 1793 in Rowan County. Their third child and second son, James Keen Jacks, was born in Rowan County on 26 September 1795, followed by daughter Lucy, around 1796.

The Family Leaves Rowan County – Following the Path of Daniel Boone to Kentucky

Just after the birth of Lucy, John Jr. and Sally moved their family to Montgomery County, Kentucky. That was about 1797. Montgomery County was just east of Lexington, Kentucky. Their next child, third son John Greenberry Jacks, was born in Montgomery County, about 1798. John Jr.'s brother Richard married Sophia Barnes in Madison County, Kentucky, in 1797, so we can see several members of the Jacks clan leaving postwar North Carolina and coming to Kentucky.

John Jr.'s father moved his family to Kentucky about this same time, also settling in Montgomery County. John Sr.'s brother Richard came with him; both John Sr. and Richard, as well as John Jr., are all found on the 1800 Montgomery County tax list. They were part of a great migration from North Carolina into Kentucky, a migration which began before the Revolutionary War. One of the first families to leave the Yadkin Valley was the family of Daniel Boone. His exploration and stories of the beautiful land beyond the mountains without question help fuel the exodus. Plenty of cheap land in Kentucky proved to be an irresistible lure, which many adventurous as well as war-weary families in the Yadkin Valley could not ignore. Without question, the future for those Americans brave enough to pull up roots and move lay to the west. Kentucky had gained statehood in 1792 – the first state west of the Appalachians. Following the Revolutionary War, patriots were rewarded for their military service with free land in Kentucky. This also helped fuel the enormous migration of which the Jacks family was a part. It should be noted that John Jr.'s uncle, Richard Rebuen Jacks, older brother of John Sr.. stayed back in Surry County North Carolina.

Five Jacks Children Born in Kentucky—John Greenberry, Mary, Elizabeth, Nicholas, and Sarah

The first child born to John and Sarah in Kentucky would be John Greenberry, fifth child and third son. Sixth child, Mary (Polly) was born about 1800 in Montgomery County. Seventh child, Elizabeth, was born about 1802 in Montgomery County. Nicholas, their eighth child and fourth son, was born about 1804 in Montgomery County. The last to be born in Kentucky was Sarah Labony or Sabaray, born about 1806 also in Montgomery County. Montgomery County, Kentucky, was created from Clark County in 1796. By the time John Jr. and Sally, plus other Jacks clan members, arrived in Montgomery County, the boom had been in progress for some time. We have no indication what type of work John Jr. was doing.

Their next child, George G. or Columbus Jacks, was born about 1810 in Overton County, Tennessee. We do not know why the family was there, but by this time we are witnessing a characteristic of John Jr. which is unique. More than the other Jacks, John Nicholas Jr. moved frequently, which has led some to speculate that John and Sarah might in some way be associated with some Baptist mission movement, as it is hard to imagine how he could be engaged seriously in farming and moving so often.

Both John Sr. and John Jr. could not possibly have escaped the effect of a religious movement labeled the Second Great Awakening. The event began in a small place in adjoining Bourbon County, known as Cane Ridge. In 1801 a large camp meeting in Cane Ridge occurred where phenomena such as "speaking in tongues" swept the crowds. This began a widespread spiritual revival which culminated in what would be called the Restoration Movement. This movement is claimed to have sparked the birth of church denominations such as Disciples of Christ, Churches of Christ, and several other lesser groups. The Jacks family would certainly have had neighbors who attended the Cane Ridge camp meeting, if they themselves had not attended. But they were living in the vicinity of the Cane Ridge meeting, and the religious revival it sparked had far-reaching effects. This might be a clue to John Jr.'s active church life, but we will probably never know for certain.

The 1810 United States Census shows a John "Jack" and family in Gallatin County, Kentucky. The ages and number of children fit with those of John Jr. so that is probably John Jr., prior to the birth of George Jacks. This John Jack is shown to own four slaves; again, there is no indication of what type of work John Jr. was doing in Gallatin.

In 1812 John and Sarah are involved in the Old Sulphur Baptist Church located in Cumberland County, Kentucky. Cumberland is just north of the Tennessee state line and close to Overton County, Tennessee, where their son George G. or Columbus was born. Old Sulphur Baptist Church records for Saturday 20 June 1812 read, "Received Sister Jacks by letter." The following month the same church records for Sunday 19 July 1812 read, "John Jacks came before the Church and the Church restores him and gives him a letter."

On 12 August 1813, John Jr. and Sarah's daughter Penelope married James Spears, neighbor and family friend. The Spears family attended church with the Jacks family. Some sources say the Spears family was associated with a school in that area also. The marriage of Penelope is the last record we have of John Jr. and Sarah's family in Kentucky. Sometime after this, they would move their family yet again, this time to Alabama.

The Jacks Family in Alabama

Sometime between Penelope's marriage in 1813 and March of 1819, John Nicholas Jacks Jr. and his wife Sarah moved again, this time to an area on the cutting edge of the westward migration. They settled in the beautiful Blount Valley, which is now inside the city of Birmingham. They built a one-room log cabin and began life anew once again. The county of Jefferson was created after they settled. The tiny community was called Five Mile Creek and had only a handful of settlers. Many knew each other as they were all coming from the same places. Once again, the Jacks family was part of a great westward migration.

It was here in the Blount Valley that John and Sarah again became associated with a Baptist church, the historic Ruhama Baptist Church. They were founding members and for a while the church met in their log cabin. Records from the Ruhama Baptist Church, now residing in the library of Samford University in Birmingham, read, "whose names are hereunto attached, the number of nine become regularly organized on the 27th of March 1819 by the assistance of our beloved Brother Hosea Holcombe who became a member with us. We constitute at the house of Mr. and Mrs. Jacks, Valley of Blount County, Alabama." Today a historic marker in Birmingham at the site of the church shows us the location of John and Sarah's cabin.

Their family of twelve children was rapidly maturing and leaving the nest. On 8 April 1819, son John Greenberry married Susannah Barton. On 9 February 1820, daughter Mary "Polly" married Leonard Coker Jr. On 29 June 1820, still another marriage; this time daughter Elizabeth to John M. Daniel, Jr. After a pause of about four years, there were two more marriages; daughter Sarah married Burwell Gragg on 4 November 1824 and son Nicholas married Sarah Harris six days later, all while John and Sarah lived in Five Mile Creek. The last of the Jefferson County weddings took place on 16 November 1829 when son George married Elizabeth Ritchly. While we can't know with certainty, probably most if not all these marriages took place in Ruhama Baptist Church. Shortly after this, John and Sarah would turn away from their life in this beautiful valley and retrace their steps back to Tennessee. We have no idea why they left.

A Reunion in Tennessee

Their trip back to Tennessee would have taken them about a month in ox-drawn carts. The decision to move surely was not undertaken lightly. To put the move into a modern-day perspective, they were living in what would later become the city of Birmingham, Alabama, and would travel by ox-drawn cart for around a month to the outskirts of Memphis, which had been founded about 10 years earlier and was still considered part of the western frontier.

If we see any pattern to these moves, it would be that they seem to always be moving to frontier areas with rapidly expanding populations. They did not go backwards, towards the east. This could indicate John Jr. was involved in some sort of commerce. Yet he often owned quantities of land suitable for farming. Some have suggested their frequent moves involved missionary work with the Baptist Church. It's doubtful we will ever know the answers. What we do know is when they settled in Fayette County, Tennessee, their neighbors were old family friends and in-laws like Claiborn Harris, George and Benjamin Spears (Speers) and son-in-law James Spears. The Spears had attended the Old Sulphur Baptist Church back in Cumberland County with John and Sarah in 1812, more than 18 years earlier.

By this time, John was about 60 and according to the 1830 United States Census all their children with the exception of their youngest, William Martin, had already left home. Since daughter Penelope had married James Spears, perhaps they moved back to be near her also. In 1835, their youngest son, William Martin, married neighbor Narcissa Temperance Redding in Fayette County. The following year, in 1836, John is recorded

as paying "1 white poll tax." This is the last record we have of
John Jr. in Fayette County. Some researchers claim he and Sarah
moved to Bedford County, Tennessee, prior to 1840 and that
they are found on the 1840 U.S. Census there. However, close
examination of the copy of the handwritten census form on the
page the researcher referred shows that the name was John
Jacobs and not John Jacks. This is the opinion of the official
transcriber and also my opinion. I viewed the entry under high
magnification and it clearly shows the name as Jacobs. We have
no census record for John and Sarah in 1840.

John and Sarah ... The Last Move—Mississippi ... Where They Will Rest

Once again, we don't know why and we don't know exactly
when, but sometime after John paid his "white poll tax" in
Fayette County, Tennessee, in 1836, he and Sarah moved to
Yalobusha County, Mississippi. Why did John and Sarah move
to Mississippi? We can only speculate. The 1840 U.S. Census
shows their son John Greenberry and his family living in
Choctaw County, Mississippi. We see where John and Sarah
purchased 160 acres in nearby Yalobusha County on 5 February
1841, for a recorded price of $20. By January 1842, records
show that son John Greenberry and wife Susannah had also
purchased land in Choctaw County. The Yalobusha County,
Mississippi, 1845 Census shows John and Sarah living there
alone. By this time John would have been about seventy-five
years old.

In 1845, apparently life on the farm had grown too much
for the aging John and Sarah; records show they sold their 160
acres in 1848 for $70. They then went to live with granddaugh-
ter Mary Cox, wife of Christopher Cox; the Coxes also lived in
Yalobusha County. Mary was the daughter of John and Sarah's

seventh child, Elizabeth. Perhaps one or both of them were not in good health. For the first time in many decades, Sarah and John would not be the head of the house they lived in.

Sarah Keen Jacks died shortly thereafter. The word would go out to many descendents in many states that their beloved matriarch had passed. She died sometime between October of 1848 when they sold the land, and the 1850 U.S. Census on 31 October 1850. We don't know Sarah's exact age but she was probably in her mid-seventies when she passed. From the time of their marriage around 1790 in Timber Ridge, Rowan County, North Carolina, John and Sarah had a full life together. They had twelve children, seven sons and five daughters, moved at least seven times, and shared a marriage lasting almost sixty years. They were founding members of the famous Ruhama Baptist Church in what is now Birmingham, Alabama, and attended numerous other frontier churches. They spent most of their life together living on the frontier. Family records indicate Sarah was buried in Torrance Cemetery, located in Yalobusha County. The historical town of Torrance and its old cemetery are now under Lake Grenada, just south of Coffeeville and east of I-55.

John Nicholas Jacks Jr. died sometime after the 1850 census. We cannot find a record of the exact date. He died in the home of Christopher and Mary Cox. Our family tradition says he was buried beside his beloved Sarah in the Torrance Cemetery. He would have been more than 80 years old. John saw the beautiful Yadkin Valley; he saw civil unrest, militias, the American Revolution, and the birth of the United States of America. Very possibly he met Daniel Boone. He saw the United States Constitution ratified. He saw the War of 1812. He saw Vermont, Kentucky, Tennessee, Ohio, Louisiana, Indiana, Mississippi, Illinois, Alabama, Maine, Missouri, Arkansas, Michigan, Florida, Texas, Iowa, Wisconsin, and possibly California admitted to the Union. He lived under twelve American presidents. The pages of

American history written during John and Sarah's life would fill a volume. Their experiences together . . . a novel. They were truly an island in an ocean of change.

CHAPTER 6

NICHOLAS JACKS

Between 1880 - 1906
Montgomery County, Kentucky

Life on the Edge of the Bluegrass Mountains

Nicholas Jacks was the fourth son and the eighth child of John Nicholas Jacks Jr. and Sarah "Sally" Keen's thirteen children. His parents, John Jr. and Sally, came to Kentucky from North Carolina sometime in 1799. They settled in Montgomery County. Nicholas's uncle Richard as well as his grandfather John Sr. had also come to Montgomery County from North Carolina. This was yet another example of how the family tended to move together, and as seen in later generations, they tended to be a part of large numbers of migrating Americans seeking new lives and fortunes mostly associated with the promises of affordable land.

At the time of their arrival in Kentucky the area was sparsely populated. The Commonwealth of Kentucky had been in existence less than eight years, and Montgomery had been a county for less than two years. They settled in what is now called the Outer Bluegrass Region of the state. The gentle hills ranged from about 700 to almost 1500 feet in elevation. The heavily forested land was extremely fertile. Indian threats by the turn of the century had substantially subsided from the significant hazards they represented a mere twenty years earlier. Kentucky was a land of promise.

Nicholas's Early Life

Nicholas was born in Montgomery County, Kentucky, about 1804. His siblings John, Mary "Polly," Elizabeth, and Sarah were all born while the family lived in Montgomery County. Little is known about Nicholas's early life. We know he grew up in a religious home. His father, John Nicholas Jr., moved the family more than usual; some have speculated Nicholas's father may have been a missionary or a minister. To date no direct evidence has been found that could confirm this; more evidence has been found supporting he was a farmer. We do know they were involved with churches in several locations where they settled, but this was common and does not by itself indicate he was a minister. For whatever reason, Nicholas and his family moved frequently during his childhood. Before his marriage at age 20, Nicholas had lived with his family in Montgomery, Gallatin and Cumberland counties in Kentucky, Overton County, Tennessee, and Jefferson County, Alabama; five moves in less than 20 years. This was unusual for those times.

Cumberland County, Kentucky

Sometime after Nicholas's sister Sarah was born in 1806, John Jr. moved his family to Cumberland County in the far south of Kentucky, just north of the Tennessee border. Again the church would play a central focus in Nicholas's life. His family would attend the Old Sulphur Baptist Church, and it was here that Nicholas's older sister Penelope would meet young James Spears, and on 12 August 1813 they would marry. Penelope was twenty. By this time Nicholas was nine; his oldest brother Thomas had married three years earlier, so Nicholas probably viewed Penelope's marriage as just a little more empty space at the supper table. Two years after Penelope married James Spears, Nicholas's older brother James Keen married Penelope's husband James's sister, Catherine Speaars. Following James Keen's marriage, Nicholas's father took the family to Alabama.

Territory of Alabama – Blount Valley

Records indicate Nicholas's parents came to Blount County, Alabama, sometime after James Keen's marriage on 17 October 1815. Alabama became a territory of the United States on 3 March 1817. It was about this time that Nicholas's parents and their dwindling family left Cumberland, Kentucky, and moved southwest into the Alabama Territory.

Ruhuma Baptist Church of Christ

Again, Nicholas's parents became active in starting a church, this time in association with a somewhat famous Baptist minister, Hosea Holcombe. The church would undoubtedly become an important part of Nicholas's life also. The new church was established on 27 March 1819. Less than two weeks later, on 8 April 1819, Nicholas's older brother John Greenberry married Susannah Barton. Most likely, the wedding was held in the Jacks home, which at the time was also the home of the church. On 14 December 1819, the territory of Alabama entered the United States as its 22nd state. Nicholas was about fifteen years old.

Even More Room at the Supper Table

Shortly after John's marriage to Susannah Barton, two more of Nicholas's sisters married; Mary "Polly" married Leonard Coker Jr. on 9 February 1820 and Elizabeth married John M. Daniel Jr. on 29 June 1820. So before summer there were two more seats at the supper table. Nicholas was now about sixteen.

Weddings Again Come in Twos

We don't know how Nicholas met Sarah Harris. We don't know how Nicholas's sister Sarah met Burwell Gragg; but the month of November 1824 brought two more weddings to

Nicholas's family. On Thursday 4 November 1824 Sarah Jacks would marry Burwell Gragg and on the following Wednesday, 10 November 1824, Nicholas Jacks and Sarah Harris would wed. Nicholas was about 20 years old and Sarah about fifteen. Since these were fall weddings, perhaps they waited till all the crops were in. We believe the two families had known each other for some time. John Jacks Jr. and his family, along with the Claiborn Harris family (father of Nicholas's wife Sarah), would leave the Alabama frontier together and travel back to Fayette County, Tennessee, not too long after the wedding. Young Nicholas and Sarah would stay and begin their life together there in Five Mile Creek, Jefferson County, Alabama.

Five Mile Creek

Nicholas and Sarah made their home in a beautiful valley filled with clear cool springs, known as Five Mile Creek. The community no longer exists but from other historical references, we can know with certainty its location; today it lies within the city of Birmingham. According to research by Dr. Ken Kirby of Samford University, the name "Five Mile Creek" refers to, "the distance from a pioneer-era creek crossing in Center Point to the old Ruhama Academy boarding school, in what is now South East Lake. The log cabin school, closed during the Civil War, was built on Second Avenue South and 80th Street in Birmingham. Five miles was the distance pioneers had to drive their wagons from a watering hole – a spring at Spring Lake – to the boarding school."

Their First Child—Larkin Harrison Jacks

By October of 1826, twenty-three months after they were married, Sarah and Nicholas had their first child, a son they named Larkin Harrison. Sarah was probably not quite eighteen and Nicholas about twenty-three. Eventually many more children would fill their home; thirteen in all.

Six Years ... Three Kids and a Farm

Nicholas and Sarah's life was busy. On 20 July 1828 their second son, William Thompson, was born (probably named for Sarah's father Claiborn Thompson Harris), followed by their third son, John Martin, about 1830. Nicholas and Sarah bought land during this time also, and census data indicates Nicholas was a farmer. Agriculture was the chief way most Jefferson County residents made their living, but the county was growing rapidly and local industry was also developing. Although we don't know for certain, it's likely Nicholas grew mostly cotton, which he would sell. He also most probably raised corn to feed his livestock. Small farms like Nicholas and Sarah's also would have had an orchard, and a few cows for milk, butter, and cream, as well as for beef. They also would have chickens and pigs, since pork was the primary meat for small farmers such as they were. Without question, this was not an easy life but Nicholas and his family appeared to be moderately successful. On such farms, everybody who was physically able worked; Larkin and William wouldn't have been exceptions.

A Land of Plenty—Plenty of Children

All of Nicholas and Sarah's children would be born in Five Mile Creek. After John Martin, their fourth son, James Keen Jacks, was born about 1835 (named for Nicholas's older brother, James Keen). Their first daughter, Mary Ann, was born about 1836, Elizabeth C. or Eliza on 16 March 1838, Mariah Frances (Fannie) about 1840, Sarah Elizabeth about 1842, Harriet Amanda (Mandy) about 1844, Lucinda E. about 1846, Abraham Nicholas about 1848, and child number thirteen, Melinda Margaret, about 1857.

By the time of the 1840 U.S. Census, Nicholas and Sarah

had eight children. The census records another adult male living with them. The census also showed that Nicholas owned two slaves, a male age 55 or older and a female between the ages of 10 and twenty-three. In May of 1841, Nicholas sold a piece of land in Jefferson County to a man named Moses Fields. Again in October of 1844 Nicholas sold another piece of land to Thomas Meares, Peter Anderson, and Earle Taylor. In 1845 John and Sarah's first child, Larkin Harrison, married Elizabeth L. Cunningham. Three years later their second son, William Thompson, married Elizabeth Jane Cannon.

The 1850 United States Census shows a significantly different picture for Nicholas and Sarah. Sons Larkin, William, John, and James had begun lives of their own. Sarah and Nicholas were at home with daughters Mary Ann, age 16, Nancy, 14, Elizabeth, 12, Mariah, 10, Sarah, 8, Harriet, 6, and Lucinda, 4. The only son at home was young Abraham who was about 2 years old. This must have made running the farm difficult for Nicholas. Sons Larkin and James Keen had decided to join the great westward migration and had gone to Chickasaw County, Mississippi. Son John Martin married Jemima Robins on 19 August 1851 and they were still in Jefferson County on a farm near her family's farm. Nicholas, unlike his father John Nicholas Jr., had stayed in one location, Five Mile Creek, for close to thirty years. But this was about to change.

Chickasaw County, Mississippi—Farewell to Five Mile Creek

Life is change; life in Mississippi brought a great deal of it. Not very long after John Martin's wedding, Nicholas and Sarah followed sons Larkin Harrison and James Keen to Chickasaw County, Mississippi. We don't know exactly when this move took place but we know by 1854 they were in Red Land, Chickasaw County. Family records indicate daughter Nancy Jane married Reuben Ricks about 1854 in Chickasaw County. By 1855, nine-year old daughter Lucinda died in Chickasaw County. The red soil of Chickasaw County would receive more of the family than just Lucinda; in 1857 Abraham Nicholas died, also at the age of nine, and daughter Sarah Elizabeth died from typhoid fever in May of 1860.

By the mid-1850s, Red Land was booming. According to an old newspaper account, "Red Land has eight stores, including a tailor shop, a tavern, a grog shop, a wheelwright's shop (wagon wheel repair), and all told, is a very handsome little place where everybody seems like they are contented and doing well." By 1842 Red Land had a post office.

The 1860 Census, taken on 2 August, showed Nicholas and Sarah living in the Red Land community with daughters Mary, 23, Eliza, 21, Fannie, 18, Mandy, 15, and Margie, 9. Nicholas at age 56 was the only male left at home. By this time Sarah was 52. The census showed Nicholas' occupation as "farmer." There is no evidence Nicholas still owned the two slaves shown on the 1840 census; the male slave, if still alive, could have been over seventy years old by then. So it's pretty certain Nicholas was trying to farm his land by himself. Sometime shortly after the census was taken, daughter Mary Ann or "Polly" married George Mathis . . . more room at the table. Through the deaths and the marriages, the ever-present political unrest hovered over everything like a dark storm cloud. It dominated the conversations and the newsprint. Nobody knew with certainty exactly what would happen but few believed anything good would come and even fewer believed it would go away.

Clouds of War—Hardship, Uncertainty, and Sorrow

While Chickasaw County lay in the heartland of the South, the county was anything but wholeheartedly in support of secession. Most residents of Red Land were not slave owners. Anti-slavery sentiment ran high in the county – but so did the issue of states' rights. In the end, states' rights trumped anti-slavery.

The country was still young and distrust of a strong federal government was strong, especially in the agriculturally based South. Nicholas's grandfather John Nicholas Jacks Sr. had fought in the American Revolution. His grandfather's brother Richard Reuben Jacks did also. Nicholas's father remembered the war as a child. They'd all heard stories about the British oppression. Nicholas and his neighbors were, for the most part, descendents of the brave patriots who fought and died to throw off the British oppression. Their fierce independence would not stand idly by while the North forced its will upon them.

From extensive research done by the Chickasaw County Historical and Genealogical Society, an in-depth view into the hardships and tragedies that existed during the war and the following period of Reconstruction has been preserved. Most of the following information about the conditions of the time was drawn from their work.

Chickasaw County's leaders, while making a statement supporting the Union, made it quite clear in a set of resolutions that if push came to shove, they would go with the South. When Jefferson Davis resigned his position in the United States Congress and Abraham Lincoln was elected President on 6 November 1860, the die was cast. In early January 1861, Mississippi held a convention in Jackson to consider secession. Delegates voted 84 to 15 to secede from the Union. Chickasaw County sent its two representatives to the convention in Jackson with a single mind. Mississippi should secede. On 9 January 1861 Mississippi became the second state, after South Carolina, to leave the Union. Others would follow in rapid succession. Chickasaw County was now very much in the war.

On January 11th, Alabama passed her secession resolution. The Alabama delegation had met in Montgomery and voted 61 to 39 for secession. By early February, three months after Lincoln's election and a month before his inauguration, seven states had left the Union. These states agreed to send representatives to Montgomery, Alabama, to form a new government. On February 8th, the delegates adopted a Provisional Constitution and the Confederate States of America were born. On February 9th, the delegates elected Jefferson Davis of Mississippi as Provisional President. Alexander Stephens of Georgia was chosen as the Confederate Vice President. On February 18th, Davis and Stephens were inaugurated as the first and last President and Vice President of the Confederacy.

On March 4, 1861, Abraham Lincoln was inaugurated as President of the United States. Two days later, the Confederacy called for 100,000 volunteers for its provisional army. On March 11th, delegates adopted the Confederate Constitution. Many men responded to the Confederacy's call. Nicholas and Sarah's son James Keen enlisted in Capt. T.H. Shackelford's Company of the Mississippi Volunteers in Okolona, Chickasaw County, Mississippi, on 27 July 1861. This company later became Company E, 4th Confederate Infantry, and also 1st Regiment Alabama, Tennessee, and Mississippi Infantry. In the 1860 Census James Keen was not married.

Next son, John Martin, would enlist on 16 September 1862. He was still back in Alabama, so Nicholas and Sarah would not be present to hug him as he went off to war. He joined Company F of the 40th Alabama Infantry, leaving his wife Jemima, and four children behind: daughters Sarah, 9, Melinda, 7, and sons James, 5, and Nicholas, 2.

Chickasaw County was the scene of several clashes during the war. The M & O Railroad was constantly targeted by Union forces. At one point Union forces entered Houston, the principal city of Chickasaw County. The local residents, in an attempt to save their county records, had loaded them onto a wagon. The

Union troops intercepted the wagon and burned everything. Two volumes that were overlooked when the wagon was being loaded are all that remained of the county's records; years of history, destroyed in a matter of moments.

The Union forces also burned stockpiles of grain which residents desperately needed to survive. Most of the county's able-bodied males were away in the war. Work fell to older men, women, children, and slaves. Most slaves in the Red Land area belonged to small farmers and according to local historical sources remained faithful to their owners. Again, according to local historical sources, it was the slaves on the larger plantations who had been abused. The economic conditions in Chickasaw County toward the end of the war had become stark; if supplies could not be grown or made on the farms they did not exist. One account relates how potato skins were parched to make "coffee." Bark and berries were used to dye cloth and make medicines.

Casualties on both sides were high; scholars estimate the dead on both sides exceeded 620,000 during the War Between the States. On both the Union and Confederate sides, disease claimed more than wounds from battle. John Martin was the first of Nicholas and Sarah's sons to die in the war. Almost immediately upon enlistment he became seriously ill. We do not know if he died from disease or from battle wounds, but by the spring of 1863 less than six months after he enlisted, John Martin Jacks was dead. On 14 May 1863 his widow Jemima applied for a Confederate widow's pension. This dispute over slavery, states' rights, or whatever history would decide to write about it had taken Jemima's husband and the father of her four children. It had taken Nicholas and Sarah's son. But the war's appetite for carnage and the lifeblood of so many was not yet appeased.

Son James Keen was captured in a long drawn-out battle for

an island in the Mississippi River known as Island No. 10. The
Confederates had held it since the beginning of the war, and had
successfully prevented the Union forces from using the
Mississippi to transport troops and supplies into the South. It
was an extremely strategic position and the Union placed a high
priority on gaining control of it. The battle lasted almost six
weeks. When the island finally fell to Union forces on 8 April
1862, James Keen became a prisoner of war, one of approximately 4,500 Confederate soldiers taken prisoner that day. The
casualties were relatively low; combined with the fact that the
fight for Island No. 10 took place at the same time as the brutal
and bloody battle of Shiloh, the Battle of Island No. 10 never
received as much attention. According to research done by
historian and author James H. Jacks-Brocker, a direct descendent
of Nicholas Jacks, James Keen was then transferred to Camp
Randall, Wisconsin, and later to Camp Douglas, Illinois. At
Camp Douglas, he became part of a 726-man prisoner exchange
and sent onboard the steamer *J.H. Done* to Vicksburg. There,
according to Jacks-Brocker, the group was reformed with
soldiers from the 50th Alabama, the 1st Alabama-Mississippi-
Tennessee Regiment, and 40th Tennessee Regiment into what
was thereafter known as the 54th Regiment Alabama Infantry.
Certainly when the news arrived back in Red Land, Nicholas
and Sarah were filled with relief.

But their joy would not endure. Once again, according to
Jacks-Brocker's research, James Keen fought with the 54th
Regiment Alabama Infantry in the battle of Jackson in July of
1863, and during the winter of 1863-1864 fought under the
command of General Braxton Bragg against the advancing Union
army of General Sherman. He fought in the battles of New Hope
Church, Pickett's Mill, and Kennesaw Mountain. At the battle of
Peach Tree Creek and Resaca they suffered heavy losses. While
defending Atlanta, his group suffered some of its heaviest losses;

on 28 July, half of their men were either killed or wounded in an assault against Union lines.

Finally, after surviving most of the war without serious injury, James Keen Jacks was captured for the second time on 3 August 1864 near Atlanta by General Sherman's 2nd Division 23rd Army Corps. As a prisoner of war, he was handed over to the Army of the Cumberland on 5 August. War records indicate he was first sent as a POW to Nashville on 11 August. Shortly afterward, still according to Jacks-Brocker's research, he was transferred to a military prison in Louisville, Kentucky. On 16 August 1864 James Keen was again transferred as a POW, this time to Camp Chase, Columbus, Ohio. Life in these prisons was worse than battle for most; thousands died from malnutrition and disease. The freezing cold and the lack of medical attention were inhuman. The war ended for James Keen Jacks on Monday 23 January 1865, seventy-four days before General Robert E. Lee's surrender on 9 April 1865. A single brief notation on his POW record read "died of pneumonia." Sarah would wipe away her tears once again; the war had claimed yet another son.

Larkin Harrison, the firstborn of Nicholas and Sarah, would also go off to war. By this time he had moved on to Arkansas; Larkin had not been among the first of those who rushed off to enlist and fight for the South, but as it became obvious his home and family were in danger, things changed. A less tangible but nonetheless real factor could have been the perhaps unspoken social pressure to go off to war. The battle was not going well and Union troops were all over Arkansas. Battles were not as numerous as they were just across the Mississippi River, only about 40 miles away, but they were still quite real. On 1 February 1863 Larkin Harrison Jacks, along with his brother-in-law James Cunningham, left Branchville in Drew County, Arkansas, and traveled about 20 miles to Monticello, the government center of Drew County, to enlist in the Confederate

Army. Both Larkin and James joined Company B, 24th Regiment, Hardy's Arkansas Infantry. Brother John Martin had already died in the war, and brother James Keen had been a POW, been released, and was about to join in a fierce battle to defend Jackson when Larkin and James Cunningham left Branchville to enlist. Sarah would certainly have many more nights of anguish and tears. Larkin was wounded in the Battle of Jenkins Ferry, but of the three sons in the war, he was the only one to come home alive. James Cunningham, Larkin's wife's younger brother who signed up with Larkin, also survived. For Sarah and Nicholas's family the war's far reaching tentacles didn't stop with John Martin and James Keen. Family records lead most to believe it also claimed the life of daughter Polly's husband, George Mathis, as well.

The War Ends – Followed not by Peace . . . But "Reconstruction"

The war's end brought little celebration for Nicholas and Sarah or any resident of Chickasaw County, Mississippi. The economy was in a shambles, carpetbaggers and scalawags were everywhere. Bands of roaming blacks became a problem. In reality, most ex-slaves had it worse than the whites, although it was the whites who were supposedly being punished by the so-called "Reconstruction." Returning soldiers found once prosperous farms in ruins; crops destroyed, most of the livestock stolen or driven away. They were broken in body and in spirit.

Chickasaw County was under military rule. Martial law was enforced by Federal troops. The plight of former slaves was even worse than that of the whites. They generally possessed nothing of material value and lacked many of the skills necessary to survive under these conditions. With the assassination of President Lincoln a more radical faction gained control of the government and a mentality of punishing the conquered

Southerners dominated government "Reconstruction" policy. Men who had served in the Confederacy were stripped of their right to vote. Political turmoil best described government in Chickasaw County. The Republican Party became the party of northern carpetbaggers, and the Democratic Party the party of southern whites. The Ku Klux Klan arose to confront these injustices but soon degenerated into a group dedicated to terrorizing blacks into not voting. It would be a long time before life would regain any normality.

Sometime during the war, daughter Elizabeth (Eliza) married Maxil F. "Mack" Evans. We can find no record of their marriage, so logically assume their marriage record was one of so many others destroyed by the Union forces on 20 April 1863 during their raid into the city of Houston. By the time of the 1880 Census, Eliza and husband Mack Evans were living in adjoining Calhoun County. Mack Evans was listed as age 43, Eliza 41, and they had six children ranging in age from 16 down to 6.

After the war and during the hardships of reconstruction, daughter Harriet Amanda (Mandy) married Johnson P. Mathis. The Mathis family lived in Red Land also. They married on 9 September 1866 but about a year later Mandy died; Mandy and John Mathis' daughter Sallie went to live with Nicholas and Sarah. Shortly after Mandy's death, Johnson Mathis married again, to Mandy's older sister, Mariah Frances (Fannie) Jacks.

Nicholas ... The Latter Years

Nicholas and Sarah were aging. As the years ticked by, their children were all leaving home. The 1870 Census finds Nicholas, age 65 – still listed as a farmer on his own land in Chickasaw County; Sarah, age 61, and youngest child Melinda, age 18. Nicholas and Sarah are also raising Sallie Mathis, the three-year-old child of their daughter Mandy, who had died just after Sallie was born. In 1871 death would knock at their door once again. This time it would be for Sarah. Sarah Harris Jacks, child bride, mother of thirteen, and Nicholas's companion in life since 9 November 1824, passed away. Together they had shared much joy, and together they had seen so much tragedy. Nicholas would never remarry. Today we can find no trace of her final resting place; the same is true for all in the Jacks family who died while in Chickasaw County. County historians agree that countless graves are lost to time, but we can say almost without question that Sarah is buried somewhere in Red Land. Local cemetery records that go back to that period are fragmented. Many grave markers in the cemetery from that period were put there many decades later, by surviving relatives who remained in the area rather than moving on as Nicholas and their children would do.

The hardships of Reconstruction dragged on. More evidence of the stark economic conditions that prevailed for Red Land's residents can be found in the 1873 Chickasaw County, Mississippi, Tax List; Nicholas paid a tax of $0.80 on his personal property listed on the tax roll as "2 hunting dogs."

But there were some good times during the evil period of Reconstruction. One of them was the marriage of Nicholas and Sarah's last daughter Melinda to Francis Craig (sometimes spelled Craige). This marriage would be significant for Nicholas. Soon afterward, the Craig family would move on westward, across the Mississippi River and into Arkansas. They would join so many of their neighbors who simply had had enough of Mississippi's harsh conditions after the war. Nicholas's oldest son Larkin was there. Many friends were settling in Drew County and its surrounding areas. Second son William was in nearby Montgomery County, along with the Mathis family. His daughter Polly had married Martin Mathis. The Clarks were there, the Cunninghams (Larkin's in-laws), the Harris family, the Cole family, all fleeing the severe economic and physical conditions left by the war.

The 1880 U.S. Census shows Nicholas, age 76, living with daughter Melinda (age 23) and her husband Francis Craig (26) in Gap Township, Montgomery County, Arkansas. Nicholas is referred to as "father-in-law" and "retired farmer." Some family stories also say Nicholas was a "tanner." This is the last reference to Nicholas anyone has been able to find. Personally, I believe his final years lie recorded in forgotten papers in some old forgotten box. Jacks family stories say Nicholas (Grandpa Jacks) lived to be over 100. Hopefully some papers will come to light someday to document his last years. My guess is that Nicholas' last years were happy.

CHAPTER 7

LARKIN HARRISON JACKS

October 1826 – 24 July 1908
Five Mile Creek

His Alabama Days

Larkin Harrison Jacks was the first child born to Nicholas Jacks and Sarah Harris. Nicholas and Sarah were married in Jefferson County, Alabama, in 1824. Larkin was born in October of 1826. He would be one of thirteen children, all born in Five Mile Creek, Jefferson County, Alabama. Five Mile Creek was breathtakingly beautiful. It was located in a valley filled with springs providing crystal clear cold water year-round. Sadly, today the area where Larkin's family cabin stood is a rundown area of Birmingham.

The Alabama where Larkin was born was quite different from today. There was no city of Birmingham. His father had come there before Alabama was a state. In 1826 when Larkin was born, Alabama had been a state for only six years. It was rapidly becoming a land of vast plantations requiring large numbers of slaves to support their cotton production. By 1830, the U.S. Census showed the state had a total population of 309,527 with 38% being slaves. Larkin would hear the adults

talk about a slave rebellion that had just taken place a little
north, in the state of Virginia. There were stories and rumors
about mobs of rebelling slaves roaming about killing all whites
they came across. He heard them talking about somebody
named Nat Turner. He listened as the adults talked about state
legislatures stripping all the blacks – both free and slave – of the
right to be educated.

As a child of twelve, Larkin would watch as all the Indians
who lived in the areas surrounding his home were removed
from their ancestral homelands and relocated to lands far to the
west, in what history now refers to as "The Trail of Tears." By
1840, according to the U.S. Census again, the state population
had grown to 590,756 of which 43% were slaves. The census
shows that Larkin's father Nicholas had two slaves; Larkin
would have known slavery firsthand and lived and worked side
by side with slaves. With only two slaves, work by all family
members was guaranteed.

Larkin's status as an only child didn't last long. Twenty-one
months later his brother William was born. His parents,
Nicholas and Sarah, would continue to have children over a
period of almost 30 years. The first three were boys so Larkin
had help with the farm work as well as playmates. While the
area was still virtually on the frontier, we do know Larkin and
his siblings were able to attend school. The census shows he
could read and write; but otherwise we know very little about
this period in Larkin's life.

Larkin Marries Elizabeth

We aren't sure how Larkin and Elizabeth L. Cunningham
met. Elizabeth was two or three years older than Larkin. The
Cunningham family lived in the area near where Larkin's parents
were living in Alabama, and then later lived next to them in
Arkansas. We are relatively certain the Arkansas neighbor was

her younger brother James or "Jim" Cunningham. According to Jefferson County, Alabama, records, Larkin and Elizabeth were married by Justice of the Peace K.H. Earwin on Sunday, 30 March 1845. Why the wedding was performed by a JP rather than a minister – like so many other details of their life – will likely never be known. Shortly after they married, their first child Nancy Jane was born.

Red Land, Mississippi

Sometime after Nancy Jane was born, Larkin and Elizabeth left the Five Mile Creek area and moved their family to an area known as Red Land in Chickasaw County, Mississippi. By 1848 Larkin was paying taxes in Chickasaw County. Red Land (now extinct but referred to in historical documents as "Redland") was not as beautiful as the valley of springs in Five Mile Creek, where they had come from. The soil was indeed red. Passages in a book entitled *The Story of Redland A Historical Sketch of the Town, School, People, and Cemetery at Redland, Mississippi* published by the Redland Cemetery Association contains some interesting insights into the early life of Larkin and Elizabeth in Chickasaw County.

The following article, first published in the *Jackson Clarion* in December of 1848, allows a clear picture of the little community where they settled.

Red Sand (first name of the town) is a prosperous little town because it is an interior trade center of a thickly settled farming area. The country around is broken and hilly, not especially fertile but nevertheless producing good crops. The greatest drawback to the growth and prosperity of Red Sand is its sticky, hilly, muddy roads which makes egress most difficult up the steep hills encountered in every direction. As if this is not enough, in protracted wet weather, the branch and creek bottoms become miry and treacherous, but life there is pleasant enough if you stay there and do not try to make egress after hard rains. Merchants use dry fall weather to stock their shelves, for importation in the winter months is most unprofitable and hazardous. Most of the farmers own no slaves and cultivate their lands by themselves . . . The people of the town are friendly and most accommodating. There is, however, a great deal of drinking, especially on Saturdays when the country people come in after their supplies and to meet their friends.

Around 1848, their second child, Lydia Frances was born, followed in 1850, by another daughter; Sarah Elizabeth, "Lizzie" – probably named after Larkin's mother Sarah. It was certainly not lost to Larkin that all these daughters were no way to work a farm. Their move to Redland was interesting because there was a family connection. Not only did Larkin and Elizabeth move to Mississippi, but so did Elizabeth's father James and her younger brother James or Jim. The 1850 U.S. Census shows James and Jim Cunningham and numerous family members living just next to each other. Jim's was the 302nd house listed on the population survey, his father's was the 303rd. Larkin and Elizabeth were the 326th. In other words, "just down the road." All were living in what the census referred to as the "Eastern Division" of Chickasaw County.

Almost all the people surrounding them on the census were from Alabama, North and South Carolina, and Georgia. They were all part of a vast westward movement. The lure of new opportunities in developing territories and states, linked with the availability of cheaper land, was causing a giant westward movement and the Jacks family and their in-laws were a part of it. We're not sure exactly when, but sometime between 1850 and 1855, Larkin's father Nicholas and his family also left Five Mile Creek back in Alabama and joined them in Chickasaw County. The move to Red Land from Five Mile Creek was about 120 miles and would have been by mule- or ox-drawn wagons down dusty or muddy roads. It would have taken several days.

Red Land was red. It was cotton and farming country. While cotton was king, and the slave population soon outnumbered the white population, plenty of small farmers like Larkin Jacks could scratch out a living from this red dirt, too. The county was booming; between 1840 and 1850, the Chickasaw County population went from 2,148 to 9,887. The number of black slaves in 1840 was 807; by 1850 the number had risen to 6,480.

Red Land Fades—The Jacks Family Goes West Again . . . to Arkansas

This boom must not have extended significantly to Larkin and Elizabeth. By this time Larkin and Elizabeth had six children. After "Lizzie" was born around 1850, Larkin and Elizabeth finally had their first son, James Martin, born on 12 October 1852. On 14 February 1855 William Robert was born, followed on 27 February 1857 by John Nicholas. We can't be sure of their reasons but a great westward migration was taking place; large numbers of families were leaving Alabama, Georgia, Tennessee, and Mississippi for Arkansas, Texas, and points west. Good land for cheap prices lay just across the Mississippi River and large portions of the population were ready to move west for it. Sometime after 1857 and prior to 1860 the family left Chickasaw County, crossed the mighty Mississippi River, and settled in what was then called Drew County, Arkansas. This marked the beginning of one of the oldest and largest clans in Arkansas. Today, the Red Land Cemetery is all that remains of the once vibrant community where Larkin and Elizabeth lived.

Just outside Pine Bluff, Arkansas, in the Harmony Missionary Baptist Church Cemetery, a majority of the people buried there are descendents of Larkin and Elizabeth. Larkin's brother William was in nearby Montgomery County. The Jacks family would call Arkansas home for generations to come.

The Wagon Train

They came to Arkansas in wagons, traveling in groups. Thus, our ancestors were part of that piece of Americana known as the "wagon train" era. Because they were farmers and because horses were expensive, they almost certainly used either mules or oxen, or perhaps both. In Larkin's day, the price for a decent mule was around $60 to $70 and they required more expensive harnesses. Almost certainly Larkin would have owned a mule team, but it's unlikely he had two pair. In addition, the mules had to be fed along the route. To carry the considerable quantity of food a mule would require for the two-week trip would take up valuable space needed for babies and household belongings needed upon arrival. In addition to that, they had to carry as much food as possible to avoid the inflated roadside prices. Of course, it was rather likely that food for the horse and mule teams was offered alongside the road if one was willing to pay the prices. Oxen, on the other hand, were much less expensive, much stronger than a mule, outperformed a mule in muddy conditions, and could feed themselves, grazing alongside the road. So probably it's safe to say Larkin and his family, being farmers, had one wagon pulled by mules, and any other wagons were pulled by teams of oxen. They could both be used on the farm. History shows the oxen were by far the most commonly used in these wagon trains.

The wagons themselves were made of wood. The "box" was normally about nine or ten feet long and four feet wide, with sides two to three feet high. The axles and tongue, referred to as "running gear," were made of well-seasoned hardwood such as hickory, ash, or oak. Many had an enclosed compartment for additional storage. The tops of these wagons were usually covered with canvas which had been treated – typically with linseed oil – to make it water-resistant. The canvas was stretched over five or six bows of wood. Hickory was preferred but on such a short trip, Larkin could have used almost anything. He could not afford to be as casual about the wheels. A broken wheel could cause multiple problems, not just to the family in the wagon, but to all those in the wagon train. Breakdowns were to be avoided and scrimping on the wheels was not wise. The wagon wheels were made of high-quality hickory and the rims were made of iron. They had to be kept greased, and historical reports indicate they were usually greased at the end of each day. For a relatively short trip such as this, large quantities of grease would be unnecessary. One wheel jack and a couple of grease buckets would have gotten the entire family group through the two-week trip. Fatback or bacon grease could also be used. The group probably combined their funds and purchased a small pool of used spare parts. They could probably sell them at the destination if they were not used.

The distance of this trip was only about 225 miles, but for Larkin and Elizabeth and their young family it probably seemed much longer. Most likely the trip took almost a month. In addition, we don't know how long they had to wait at the river crossing. Generally back then the wagon trains did not travel on Sunday. This allowed the animals and the people time to regain their strength. The most one could hope for with ox-drawn carts was about ten miles per day. Mules could go a little bit faster and horse-drawn wagons slightly faster still. But by traveling in large caravans, they were stuck moving at the pace of the oxen. Sometimes in the larger groups, some men and horse-drawn wagons would head up the caravan and move on ahead at a faster pace to prepare the spot where they would rest for the night. We don't know if they had any horse teams, but being farmers, probably they did not.

The wagons would be full of belongings and supplies; everyone able to walk had to do so. Almost certainly they traveled with many other families doing the same thing and the group almost certainly included Cunninghams, Elizabeth's relatives. While we don't know for sure, they probably traveled during early summer when the rainfall would be lower allowing easier going on the dirt roads. This would also allow them time to build shelter before the winter months arrived. But the price of avoiding the rain was the heat and humidity. History reports that in addition to cheap land across the Mississippi, some moved west just to get out of the climate of heat, humidity, and disease.

The routes they most probably traveled would have been the most popular and safer. At some point, the route had to lead to a major river crossing point; they probably crossed just south of Greenville, Mississippi. There were normally places along the route about every ten to fifteen miles where travelers could spend the night in safety, and buy supplies. These areas were little more than clearings alongside the road with what amounted to "roadside stands" selling goods at inflated prices. Sometimes small communities would spring up along these areas. It's almost certain they passed through several small towns along the route in addition to these rest areas. They were heading toward a "frontier," not passing through one. This area of Mississippi had been settled years ago. To the adults, the trip could probably be described as torturous. Very likely for the Jacks children, ranging in age from about fourteen to William Robert aged about four, it appeared more of an adventure. Young John Nicholas would have been an infant.

The River Crossing

Crossing the Mississippi could have been a little frightening for them. Unless some of the men had gone on before to check out the land and build some type of shelter for the families, none would ever have seen a river this large. They probably reached the river a little over two weeks after leaving home. They could have waited as long as several days for their turn to load their wagons, livestock, and families on the barge. Records show fares of five cents per person in other areas of the Mississippi River, but no fare structure could be found for the area where their group crossed. Steam-powered ferries were in use by then, but plenty of flatboats remained. It's uncertain if they went by steam-powered vessel. As they pushed the last wagon onto the barge, and as the last animal and family member stepped aboard, the Jacks family crossed another milestone – a journey to new homes and new lands to the west. Some would remain east of the Mississippi and others would soon follow Larkin and Elizabeth, but their historic journey had begun.

Arkansas ... The New Ancestral Home

When the barge bumped the shore on the west bank of the Mississippi, they stepped into Arkansas. There had to have been excitement, perhaps even a small celebration – but for sure it didn't last long. Wagons, teams, animals – everything had to be quickly unloaded and moved away from the barge. New cargo was waiting to be loaded for the trip back across to Mississippi.

Larkin and his family would leave the river and head north-west toward Monticello. There were still plenty of farms and plantations; the river was the center of everything in the area. But as they moved on away from the delta everything thinned out. They were still traveling a major road; close to that road life would be very much like it had been in Mississippi. All the people who lived in the area had made the same westward migration they were making . . . only earlier. While the realization that they were now in Arkansas may have made them feel a little closer to their destination, they still had more than 75 miles to go before reaching their new "promised land" in Branchville. This last leg of their journey would take them more than a week.

Drew County

After a few days their wagons would enter the recently formed Drew County. The center of government was called Monticello, believed to be named for the famous home of Thomas Jefferson. At that time, the population of Monticello was less than eight hundred. They probably spent a day or so there before moving on. This would be the last population center of any size they would see for some time. From Monticello, they continued north toward the settlement known today as Star City, about 25 miles away. They were approaching areas more unsettled than anything they had seen in Mississippi. Forests were everywhere and wild game reported to be plentiful. They were no longer on the heavily-traveled roads they had used since leaving Mississippi. The family, although tired, must have been excited. We don't know if they continued north to the small settlement which is today Star City or if they turned northwest, on what is now called Old Military Trail. Probably they took the Old Military Trail route. If so, they would have left the main road about three miles south of Star City and headed more or less westerly and straight for Branchville. Having just come from Monticello, the largest town in the area, there would have been little need for them to have gone on to Star City.

While they were, in fact, moving into a sparsely populated area, Drew County had a rapidly growing population. The population of the county in 1850 was 3,276. But given the large area of Drew County then (county boundaries changed significantly during Reconstruction), the area was considered remote. In addition, most of the county's population was concentrated in the eastern part of the county, in and around Monticello.

This would soon change. Larkin and the Cunninghams, like so many others, were moving westward from Georgia, the Carolinas, Alabama, and Mississippi in search of cheap fertile land and the chance to create a more promising future. People were arriving daily; by 1860 the population of Drew County had reached 9,087. In many ways, this population growth was creating economic opportunities for everyone. As the government made more public lands available at cheap prices, more money flowed into the government coffers. The federal government in Washington had realized the importance of populating the country from the east coast to the west coast and was busy encouraging this westward migration. The Jacks family was part of this important phase in United States history.

Branchville ... Their New Home

Branchville would be their new home. For most of the children, this would be where they grew up. Their last child, Martin Andrew, would be born in Branchville. Sarah Elizabeth, James Martin, and William Robert would marry there, and both Elizabeth, Larkin's wife, and Andrew their son would also be buried in Branchville. Branchville would be home for a long time. Branchville itself was not much more than a handful of small stores which had sprung up to supply the needs of the settlers who were moving in, all along a reddish-brown dirt road known today as Branchville Road. A post office was located in one of the stores. Today a home still stands along Branchville Road which local residents say was once a stage depot. The house is constructed of large logs which had been trimmed to have flat surfaces. Looking at the outside of this home, one would never guess its history. Virtually everything associated with the little community has been erased by time. There is little remaining to even hint that a community once existed here; no community, no post office, only a small well-maintained cemetery, out in a pasture accessible only by driving over the grass. It was once called Norton Cemetery. Today it's called Jones Cemetery; Branchville's only residents reside here.

Their New Life

Soon Larkin and his family would be farming. They had eighty acres and a house full of people. By the time of the 1860 census (on 8 July), 15 people were under their roof, including their last son, Andrew Martin, whom the census recorded as being six months old. In addition to Larkin and Elizabeth and their seven children, a 24-year-old "farmer" named J.F. Jenkins lived with them as well as the seven members of the T.W. Clark family. We have no certain explanation for this; although one possibility could be they were newly arrived and still settling in. By the 1870 census they are no longer in the household but the Clark family did not go far; Larkin and Elizabeth's son William Robert would marry T.W.'s daughter, Martha Jane Florence Clark, in 1876.

War and Rumors of War

Secession and war came as no surprise to anyone in Branchville. It had dominated all conversations for months. The local newspapers which arrived regularly at the Branchville store were full of news about the situation. Larkin, like many others in the State of Arkansas, was not enthusiastic about the secessionist cause. They basically wanted to see Arkansas remain part of the United States. The 1860 census showed Arkansas with a population of 435,450 of whom 111,115 were slaves and only 11,481 were slave-owners. A common expression among the men in Branchville was, "rich man's battle, poor man's fight."

That soon changed when the fighting at Fort Sumter broke out. They did not like what was happening to the South; they were, after all, Southerners. Almost everyone in the area had been part of the great migration from the southern states east of the Mississippi. When you examine the Branchville area census, almost all were from Tennessee, Alabama, Georgia, North and South Carolina, and Mississippi. But outside the Branchville area, it was not uncommon to find Union sympathizers. Later during the war, several Union regiments were organized and fought against the Confederacy.

In February 1861 the Provisional Confederate Constitution was adopted. Arkansas state troops took over the Federal Arsenal at Little Rock. On May 6, 1861, Arkansas left the Union and joined the Confederate States of America. Immediately men began enlisting to fight. Arkansas formed at least 48 infantry regiments as well as numerous artillery and cavalry units. For a state with such a small population, Arkansas provided a disproportionate number of soldiers. We will never know with certainty Larkin's feelings about the war but by looking at the facts we have today, we can draw some conclusions. In May of 1861, Arkansas seceded. From that point forward men from Arkansas began enlisting in the Army of the Confederacy in significant numbers. Larkin was not among that number; he remained on his eighty-acre farm in Branchville. We do not know how many of his neighbors decided to do the same. As the war raged on, the South suffered significant defeats. While most major battles were fought outside Arkansas, many bloody battles were taking place within the state. In every edition of the newspaper, Larkin would read of more destruction, both in his state and back in Alabama and Mississippi where his relatives were. His father Nicholas was still in Chickasaw County, Mississippi. His brothers James and John were fighting with Alabama regiments. Larkin's brother James had enlisted in July of 1861. By March of 1862, James had been captured and spent time as a POW in Camp Randall in Wisconsin and later in Camp Douglas, Illinois. He was released in a prisoner exchange after about five months and immediately rejoined the struggle. Now letters from back home were saying they feared he had been captured again, after a battle near Atlanta. Larkin's other brother, John, was fighting with Alabama's 40th Infantry, Company F. Letters from his wife Jemima said he was reported sick and later reported dead. In late November and early December of 1862, heavy fighting was taking place north of Fort Smith at a small place know as Prairie Grove. Casualties on both sides were heavy. Reports estimated the Confederate forces lost over 1,300 men. The Yankees were advancing deeper into Arkansas.

Possibly the event giving the final nudge was a strategically significant battle fought at Arkansas Post, only 35 miles from Larkin's home. In this battle, five thousand vastly outnumbered Confederate forces were overwhelmed by more than 30,000 Union troops. The battle was fought on 10 January 1863. This loss gave the Union forces control of the Arkansas River, a vital strategic asset. It was also a demoralizing blow to the Confederate forces in Arkansas. Three weeks later, Larkin left home and traveled to Monticello, the county seat of Drew County, and enlisted as a private in the Confederate Army. On 1 February 1863, Lt. Col. Whittington assigned Larkin to company B of Hardy's Regiment. Almost immediately Hardy's Regiment was consolidated with portions of Dawson's Regiment and survivors of the Arkansas Post battle from Crawford's Infantry Battalion. The vast majority of Company B's soldiers were all from the Drew County area and enlisted in Monticello, just as Larkin had done.

When Larkin left home to join the battle, he was 37 years old. His oldest son, James Martin, was twelve years old. William

Robert was eight. Keeping things running on the farm was going to be a problem. Elizabeth's family lived close by so there would have been help from the Cunninghams also. But not from her brother James . . . he enlisted in Company B on 1 February 1863 with Larkin. They left home together to join the fight. This gives insight into the mindset that must have prevailed in Branchville . . . a mindset of desperation and fear.

Company B saw lots of action. They participated in the Red River Campaign and fought in the famous Battle at Jenkins Ferry in April of 1864. Larkin was wounded during this fierce battle in which many on both sides lost their lives. As the Battle of Jenkins Ferry began, the troops on both sides were already exhausted. Due to a forced march in constant rain, the men of Company B had not eaten a meal in days. Some of them carried several day-old scraps of bread in their pockets. They marched in ankle-deep mud. Their uniforms were soaked and the temperatures during the night would fall to the low 50s, producing a miserable chill. They were, however, able to have coffee before the battle began.

Company B caught up with the Union forces they had been pursuing just as the Union troops were in the process of trying to get their supply wagons and artillery across the rain-swollen creek. The Union forces had a pontoon-type bridge and were using it to get across. But because they were nowhere near getting everything across, they were forced to make a stand at the river. Larkin and the men of Company B were not in an enviable position from which to launch an attack. It was necessary for the attacking forces to pass through a clearing with high, dense, and impassable forest on both sides. The clearing was narrow and would only allow limited numbers of the attacking troops from Company B to pass at a time. This placed Larkin's company at a strategic disadvantage. The fighting was intense. Descriptions from participants reported visibility was

severely reduced due to fog and smoke from the rifles. Because
of the mud, the cavalry and artillery were basically useless. The
cavalry dismounted and fought on foot. Larkin's company was at
an additional disadvantage as the only way to see anything was
to crouch down low close to the ground. This made a rushing
attack extremely difficult. The Union defenders were not trying
to move but merely trying to hold their position, providing
cover for the wagons and artillery to get across the creek. All
they had to do was stay low and fire into the narrow area where
Company B's men were being forced to pass. Muskets roared for
over six hours. The dead and wounded were everywhere. No
serious ground was taken by either side; small shifts backwards
and forward took place, but survivors said the entire battle
never shifted more than 250 yards. Visibility was so bad that
sometimes soldiers were forced to fire at musket flashes rather
than actually seeing an enemy. The deaths were not confined to
those firing muskets.

Generals on both sides lost their lives. The carnage was
unforgettable; many survivor accounts have been preserved, all
testifying to the horror of the event. A Confederate private
remembered the battlefield after the fighting ceased:

> After the battle a detail of men were employed in
> burying the dead. Armed with shovel, pick ax, and spade
> they proceeded along the road to complete this mournful
> task which the enemy was unable to accomplish. The
> ground was thickly strewn with ghastly, mangled forms.
> It was almost too horrible for human endurance. No
> conception of the imagination, no power of human
> language could do justice to such a horrible scene.

According to Confederate Army records, Larkin was
wounded in the left hand during this battle. For this, three years

before his death, he would be awarded a military pension. Most probably the wounds he carried in his mind were more severe than the wounded hand. Both he carried to his grave.

Larkin Comes Home from War — Post-War and Reconstruction Years in Branchville

In April of 1865 Larkin was honorably discharged and returned to Branchville. We know little about his personal life for the next fifteen years. We know he already owned land, and assume that he lived and worked that land and was an active member of the small Branchville community. We do know that during the next few years, Larkin and Elizabeth's family was maturing. They were getting married, moving out, and starting families of their own. In 1868, their second daughter, Sarah Elizabeth, married James Nugent. In 1871, their first son, James Martin, married Amanda Bailey (some records show Amanda's family name as Hawkins). And in 1876 second son William Robert married Martha Jane Florence Clark; for a period of time when they were children, they had lived under the same roof. John Nicholas, their third son would marry another neighbor, Elizabeth Owens, in 1877.

But it was not all weddings. Their last son, Martin Andrew, born about 1858 – their only child to be born in Arkansas – died in early childhood. We do not know exactly when he died but he only appeared on one census, that of 1860. He almost certainly would have been buried in the small cemetery near their home called Norton.

Elizabeth ... "The Missing Years"

Sometime between the 1860 and the 1870 Census, Larkin's wife Elizabeth disappeared. We don't know where she went (if anywhere) and we don't know why. On the 1870 Census a woman named Frances – no last name given, which is how all in the same home by the same last name are shown . . . indicating her last name was Jacks – appeared immediately under Larkin's name. This is where Elizabeth had always appeared on all the previous censuses. This is where the census takers always placed the wife. Frances's place of birth was listed as Georgia, and her age as 23. Larkin's age on the same census was shown as 45. Larkin had a younger sister named Mariah Frances who would have been about that age, but she was born in Five Mile Creek, Jefferson County, Alabama, like all Larkin's other siblings. "Frances" would have been younger than Larkin's oldest child. From today's vantage point . . . Elizabeth simply disappeared. If she truly was gone everyone knew at the time, but obviously it wasn't something anyone bothered or chose to record.

Several scenarios come to mind . . . all pure speculation. The war took a toll on many marriages. It was not uncommon for men to come home from war and find their wives gone, or with child from a neighbor or even a brother or other family member into whose care she had been placed while he was away. The stress of trying to hold the farm and family together could have adversely affected her. The death of her youngest child, Martin Andrew, could also have been a factor. Or Larkin could have come home from battles like Jenkins Ferry significantly affected by the images of carnage he had seen. Today such conditions have a name – Post Traumatic Stress Disorder, but in Larkin's time there was no name for it and no help. They just suffered. Or perhaps she had simply gone to spend a few days with her family who lived close by (the Cunninghams). These censuses were always full of inaccuracies. All this, however, is merely speculation; all searches trying to locate Elizabeth during this period failed to find her. But by the 1880 Census, she is back and Frances is gone. This does not indicate ten missing years; If Elizabeth had been away, she could have returned the day after the census-taker came.

There were other interesting things appearing on that 1880 census. Nancy Jane, their first child, age 34, was shown still living at home. Her name appears as Jacks so we could assume she had not yet married. Her younger sister Lydia is also shown still living at home at about age 30. Also, daughter Sarah Elizabeth, age 28, who married James Nugent about 1868, is recorded as now living with Larkin and Elizabeth along with Lizzie's three-month-old daughter Ada. The census made no mention of Lizzie's husband James Nugent. Yet the 1900 Census shows Lizzie and her husband James Nugent living just down the road from where Larkin and Elizabeth lived. The census records they had been married 32 years. They had a house full of kids and a grandchild. What if she had just come to visit her parents for a few days? If we can learn something from this it might be that Elizabeth wasn't "missing." We will never know.

Elizabeth's Last Years

Elizabeth's last years have also been obscured. The 1890 U. S. Census was destroyed by a fire in Washington, D.C. on 10 January 1921. While a few pages survived the fire, none contained the Arkansas census; therefore, clues pertaining to Elizabeth are scarce. What we do know is that while she appeared on the 1880 Census as the wife of Larkin, by the time of the 1900 Census, she had died. Our family sources say Elizabeth died while the family was still living in Branchville, sometime between 1880 and 1899. Family sources say she was buried in Norton Cemetery (now Jones Cemetery) near their home, probably beside her son, Martin Andrew. Larkin never remarried; years later, he would be brought back and laid to rest beside them.

Larkin Moves to Whiteville – His Final Years

As his house emptied and his children began families of

their own, as his aging body began to tire, Larkin accepted an offer to come live with his third child and oldest son, James Martin, who lived about 18 miles away in adjoining Jefferson County. Around age 72, Larkin left the land he had lived on since he and Elizabeth made their way west from Mississippi more than forty years earlier. He still had to make the trip by wagon but this time the responsibilities were not on his shoulders. His sons J. M., Bob, and John Nicholas, would take care of the details.

They arranged for a neighbor and fellow Harmony Baptist Church member George H. Hunt and his wife Ada to sell Larkin 40 acres adjoining James Martin. Larkin moved into J.M.'s home. He would spend the rest of his years here surrounded by his son, Sarah, his second wife (Mandy had died shortly after their son Andrew Douglas was born in 1887), and at least eight children. This must have reminded Larkin of his early years when he and Elizabeth were raising their seven young children. It was probably a good time in Larkin's life.

Records show that in 1905 Larkin applied for a Confederate Veteran pension. On 21 July 1905, at age 79, based on the report of Dr. B. F. Traver, and predicated upon the injury to his left hand received in the Battle of Jenkins Ferry, Larkin was awarded 75% disability. This was supported by the testimonies of J. B Hegwood and N. R. Owen, both citizens of Lincoln County, who had known Larkin for 42-45 years and had firsthand knowledge of his service in Company B of Hardy's Regiment, 19th Arkansas Infantry.

Larkin Goes Home

Larkin's last years were probably generally happy . . . surrounded by loved ones. His son J. M and Sarah were active in the Harmony Missionary Baptist Church; very likely Larkin attended services with them. But as his almost 83-year-old body began to acknowledge its mortality, he may have found himself missing Elizabeth and the old family place back in Branchville. On Friday morning, 24 July 1908, Larkin passed away in the home of James Martin. On Saturday 25 July Larkin went home to Branchville for the last time . . . probably by wagon and accompanied by large numbers of family, church family, and friends. After a long, hot 18-mile trip by wagon down dirt roads, the procession would have finally turned onto Branchville Road. When they reached the Norton home place, they would turn left and move through the field up to the top of the slight hill, stopping under the shade of large oak trees. There they would lay Larkin Harrison Jacks, beside his wife Elizabeth and son Martin Andrew.

The *Pine Bluff Graphic* edition of 25 July 1908 on page 5 would print his obituary as follows: "OLD SETTLER HAS PASSED AWAY. L.H. Jacks, aged 83, one of the early settlers of Jefferson County, died at his residence near Pine Bluff Friday morning. He is well-known throughout the county. His is survived by three sons, Robert Jacks of Hope, Jim and John Jacks of Jefferson County, and one daughter, Mrs. S. Nugent. The interment will be at the old family burying ground in Lincoln County this afternoon."

CHAPTER 8

JAMES MARTIN "J.M." JACKS

12 October 1852 – 8 July 1923
Chickasaw County, Mississippi

The Days before Arkansas

In Mississippi during the 1850s, cotton was king. The cotton gin enabled Mississippi plantations to drastically increase production while using less manpower (slaves). While this was good for the larger plantation owners, it drove up the price of land, pushing it further out of reach for poorer white farmers. Society was sharply divided along the socioeconomic lines of the wealthy plantation owners, smaller white farmers and merchants, poor subsistence farmers, and slaves. James Martin was born into the small white farmer group, in the small community of Red Land in the rural area of Chickasaw County, Mississippi, on 12 October 1852. The little community of Red Land long ago ceased to exist. Today only obscure references remain of what was a community with over five hundred residents. Parts of what was the Red Land Community now are in Pontotoc County. The community's cemetery still remains, but it is now call Redland – not Red Land.

James Martin was the fourth child and first son born to

Larkin Harrison and Elizabeth "Eliza" Jacks. Larkin brought his family to the Red Land area in Chickasaw County shortly after 1845. We can speculate that James Martin was probably spoiled a bit by his three older sisters. Without doubt, he also learned at a very early age about the chores and never-ending work associated with farm life. No matter how full of warmth his home was, these were turbulent times for Mississippi.

The Mississippi of 1850 was in some ways booming. Of the state's 606,526 residents, 309,878 or 51% were slaves. The only way Europe's insatiable appetite for American cotton could be appeased was through the cruel and highly divisive institution of slavery; money poured into Mississippi from its cotton exports. But not all white farmers shared in the prosperity; a single slave cost many times more than James Martin's family land. We can find no records indicating his family ever owned slaves. The Alabama 1860 Slave Census records do indicate his uncle James Keen Jacks owned several slaves. His grandfather Nicholas had also owned slaves.

Rumors of War

Nobody knows for sure why Larkin and his wife Eliza decided to take their family and move to Arkansas; perhaps life across the Mississippi River appeared to hold more promise. There was talk of cheap land and a life free from the "cotton plantation economy" that seemed to have a stranglehold on everything around them. It was said the people in Arkansas were not gripped with the secession fever, which had reached epidemic proportions there in Mississippi. Their reasons, whatever they were, are now lost to time; all we know for sure is they left Chickasaw County, crossed the Mississippi River, and settled near another small community no longer in existence called Branchville, in what is now part of Lincoln County, Arkansas. As the crow flies, their new home was only 162 miles from all the graves they had left behind in Mississippi, but to young James Martin, it must have appeared to be a new world.

Branchville

From the 1860 census we learn that many people living in Mississippi and Alabama were moving to the Mill Creek Township area of Arkansas. Larkin's wife Elizabeth's family may have settled here too. We are not certain at this point but there were numerous Cunninghams recorded in the census living nearby Larkin's family. This would not be surprising as it was common for families to move westward in groups. After the death of James Martin's grandmother, Sarah Jacks, in 1871, his grandfather Nicholas would also leave Chickasaw County, and come to Arkansas. James Martin's new community had a small post office and some small stores on a reddish-brown dirt road. This served as the community center for Branchville. Today, all evidence of the vibrant little community once located there is gone, leaving barely a trace. Its sole epitaph . . . a dirt road named Branchville.

Eighty Acres and a Mule

James Martin's father, Larkin, soon bought eighty acres of land and the family settled in to scratch out a living in the reddish-brown soil of Arkansas's piney woods. Today this Arkansas region is known as the Timberlands. In many ways, it resembled the land back in Mississippi and James Martin adapted quickly to cutting down the pine trees that grew every-where on this new land. From these trees, the family would mill the boards to build their home or sell or trade the felled trees for already milled lumber. Most communities had a saw mill nearby. There was much work to be done in order to get their new home ready to live in, their new land cleared, and ready to yield crops to support them. Shelter for themselves, shelter for the livestock, smoke houses, animal pens-everything needed to be built. Fruit orchards, gardens, and crops had to be planted. Endless work awaited young James Martin as he moved into Arkansas and into adolescence. He was large and well-built for his age and this would serve him well in this new land where physical strength played such an important role.

He already knew what happened to those not strong enough to resist the fevers, infections, and complications of childbirth; his older brother, Abraham, died at age nine. His aunt Lucinda (only four years older than he) died at fourteen. Another aunt, Sarah, died from typhoid at eighteen. The red land of Chickasaw County, Mississippi, also would soon claim his grandmother. The land he now walked on in Branchville would receive the body of his little brother Martin Andrew before he reached twelve. James Martin would help bury him. There was not much forgiveness in these piney woods; yet, it would be all James Martin would ever know.

The Reality of War

Whenever men came together, talk of secession soon arose. In most of the conversations young James Martin would over-hear, the men were generally opposed to secession and the war. His family had no slaves. Their neighbors had no slaves. Most men outright said they didn't want to go to war to protect some rich man's plantation. The reasons being given for joining any war effort appeared unrelated to anything central to their Jacks family farm. As a young adolescent male, he might have occa-sionally entertained some romantic thoughts of defending his home in the uniform of the new Confederacy, but basically, it was not his fight. Countless times he would overhear men saying this was "a rich man's war and a poor man's fight." The farm could not survive long without his father. The eleven-year-old James Martin, though large and strong for his age, could not possibly keep the place going long without his father's presence. Both planting and harvesting had to be done within a relatively narrow window of time. Undoubtedly he worried about this.

The entire state was in political turmoil. Either slavery or anti-slavery dominated every aspect of the political spectrum. Everybody had an opinion. It was like some consuming disease. This unrest helped give birth to the Republican Party in Arkansas. Although divided on the issue of secession, President Abraham Lincoln's action against the seceding states rapidly united the majority of the state in favor the Southern cause and on 6 May 1861 Arkansas seceded and cast its lot with the Confederacy. Arkansas was at war.

James Martin's Father Enlists in the Confederate Army

James Martin's father, Larkin Harrison, managed to stay out of the war for almost two years but finally, on 1 February 1863, he left home and journeyed 23 miles south to Monticello, Drew County, Arkansas. There he enlisted for three years in the Army of the Confederate States of America. In order to manage while Larkin was away, the family could have pooled manpower with neighbors. The Cunninghams owned land nearby. These were probably the uncles of James Martin, his mother's brothers. The Cunningham family had both James, who was on the census as household # 95, and Robert listed as household # 87. The Jacks household was # 79, so obviously they were neighbors. Thankfully the war only lasted two more years but the hardship was very real to all in Branchville.

One relatively minor battle (officially classified as a skirmish) was fought in the immediate area. It took place almost on their property; not only was the hardship real, but the war itself. On 19 January 1864, Union forces, consisting of the Fifth Kansas, First Indiana, and Seventh Missouri cavalries, and led by Colonel Powell Clayton, were moving southward from Pine Bluff toward Monticello. They encountered a Confederate encampment at Branchville. After a while, the Confederate forces ceased firing and pulled back into the woods. The Union forces elected not to pursue, later claiming low ammunition. But in reality, the Union forces probably realized it was a ploy by the Confederates – familiar with every tree in the woods – to draw them into a trap. The Union forces wisely elected to return to Pine Bluff.

Civil War historians say both sides had scouting parties, moving throughout the countryside, not only looking for enemy movements but also foraging for food and supplies. In many cases, they would take all or most of the livestock they could find. Obviously this had to be a significant problem for all the families in the area.

War Ends but "Reconstruction" Begins

James Martin's father came home after the war but not to peace. Massive civil unrest would come with the "carpetbaggers," "scalawags," and unelected recently freed slaves assuming public office. New counties were created, political redistricting was common, and work was hard to find. Larkin Harrison and all the other men who had served in the Confederacy were stripped of their right to vote. The Ku Klux Klan took hold rapidly in response to disenfranchisement as well as in retaliation to the Northern-controlled legislature backed by the Union Army. Through all this, James Martin worked hard on the family farm, attended local schools. He probably became an "adult" long before his time. He could not escape being shaped by the experiences he was encountering during Reconstruction.

One good thing to come from Reconstruction was a system of free public schools. James Martin no doubt benefited from this development. We don't know the extent of his education, but census data shows he could read and write.

Romance in the Piney Woods

James Martin found time from his chores and school assignments to meet a young neighbor named Amanda "Mandy" Bailey; perhaps it was at church, maybe at a social gathering, or possibly at school. At some point the friendship became a romance. Certainly the details must have been lovingly repeated countless times over the years; those details now are gone or buried in some old forgotten box of letters. We would know little of this, had it not been noticed while doing census research, that Mandy's parents John C. (probably Calvin) Bailey, his wife Henrietta, and their numerous children were neighbors of the Jacks family. They both lived in Mill Creek Township. How long the relationship remained in the courtship stage is unknown but on Saturday, 30 December 1871, James Martin Jacks and Amanda L. Bailey were married.

Children and Changes

It's doubtful there was any sort of honeymoon. As a matter of fact, the 1880 census shows them, some nine years later, still living with Mandy's parents, the Baileys. However, by the time the census taker knocked at the door, James Martin and Mandy had four children: Calvin James, born in 1873, Charles Larkin in 1875, Albert in 1876, and in 1878, their first daughter, Cora Amanda. Calvin was named for Mandy's father and Charles Larkin for James Martin's father Larkin. The Bailey/Jacks household had eleven members. Grandparents would play a big role in James Martin and Mandy's family.

To James Martin, life was basically synonymous with hard work. Everybody was aware of life outside Mill Creek Township but there was little time to think much about it. Star City, the county seat, about four and a half miles up the muddy roads, had a local newspaper, and a copy was always available at the Branchville stores. From there James Martin could learn about events outside Branchville. By mid-1881 the *Pine Bluff Commercial*, a weekly printed on a hand-cranked press, was making its way to Branchville also. This offered a window to the world outside the little microcosm of Branchville. By this time, James Martin was more than thirty years old. He read about James A. Garfield's controversial election as President of the United States and then several months later he would read about his assassination by a lawyer named Charles J. Guiteau. He undoubtedly read about the famous outlaw Jesse James being shot to death by Robert Ford, a member of his own band, for a $5,000 reward.

The reddish-brown dirt roads offered passage to the world outside Branchville. Certainly there would be trips to Star City, the county seat, probably on Saturdays and probably via wagon pulled by a team of mules. The trip would take about two hours each way. The Star City square would be an exciting place for everybody; a place to talk to farmers from other parts of the county, and a place to look at – and on rare occasions – purchase items considered impractical to keep on the shelves of the small Branchville stores.

But life for James Martin and Amanda was not all about work, Branchville's "social life," and stories from the newspapers. While living with Mandy's parents, the Baileys, James and Mandy had managed to acquire property of their own. Records show they sold a piece of land in 1881. Also in 1881, a second daughter, Sarah Emma Jacks, was born. Sarah was named for James Martin's grandmother Sarah Harris or for his older sister Sarah Elizabeth. In 1884 William Claudis was born, Thomas Grover in 1885, and finally Andrew Douglas in 1887. By the time Andrew Douglas arrived, Mandy had given James Martin eight children in 15 years. Mandy's home must have been like a bee hive.

Heartbreak Comes To Branchville

Shortly after Andrew Douglas was born, Mandy died. The details of her death are no longer known; the likeliest probabilities point to complications of childbirth, typhoid, or infectious disease. Like the details associated with the cause of her death, the exact location of her grave has similarly vanished. Our family historical records indicate Amanda was buried in what was then called Norton Cemetery. Unfortunately, her grave is no longer marked. Unless a map or old index of the cemetery's graves is discovered, her many descendents can only know within a few yards where her final resting place was. The practice of embalming had begun to spread during the Civil War but due to their rural location, Mandy's body was probably not embalmed, so she would have to have been buried shortly after her death. She was almost certainly laid in a pine box, and kept in the coolest room of the house, usually the living room, long enough to allow family and friends to come pay final respects.

Norton—the Longest Walk

Mandy's casket would have been taken from the home down the either muddy or dusty Branchville Road. A funeral procession with pallbearers carrying her casket or the casket carried in a wagon drawn by a team of mules would have been followed by neighbors and family walking behind. The procession would slowly make its way to the tiny cemetery located about four hundred feet from the road. Probably young William and Thomas were carried in the arms of their older brothers or rode in the wagon. They would slowly make their way up the path leading to the high spot where the cemetery was located. A small stand of trees would provide shade or shelter as they reached the cemetery. The mound of fresh dirt and the opening in the ground waiting to receive their mother would just add to their gloom. They would have either hired some men, or men from the church and neighbors helped dig her grave. The family could have taken some amount of relief from their sorrow, however, in the fact that unlike today, death was common. They were all acquainted with death firsthand, since it occurred often. Infant mortality was high, death from fevers was high. Without antibiotics, infections regarded as trivial today claimed many lives. When visiting these old cemeteries, the first thing that strikes you is the disproportionate number of children's graves.

Without any doubt, the presence of their maternal grandparents in the home and nearby paternal grandparents helped ease some of the family's sorrow. For Calvin,14, Charlie, 12, Albert, 11, Cora, 9, Sarah, 6, William, 3, and Thomas, 2, their mother was suddenly gone. James Martin found himself a widower with eight children, ranging in age from 14 to newborn – and without the woman who had been his partner in life for the past fifteen years.

Sarah Lucinda

Sarah Lucinda Wortham's early life probably wasn't what you would call "story book." The 1870 United States Census first showed five-year-old Sarah living with her thirty-year-old mother, Dorcas. Her mother appeared to be the head of the family. They lived in the gently rolling hills and piney woods of Dallas County, Arkansas, approximately 60 miles from where James Martin and his family were living. On 17 July 1881, Sarah married Anson B. Strait. She was only fifteen years old. This marriage took place in Jefferson County. Thirteen months later she had her first child, Thomas Albert Strait, on 10 August 1882. From later documentation, we know Thomas had gray eyes and brown hair. Shortly after he was born, Anson B. Strait died, leaving the seventeen-year-old Sarah a widow.

On 21 April 1883, Sarah married John L. Sikes. This marriage shows both Sarah and John Sikes as residents of

Redfield, a small community in far northwest Jefferson County,
which had sprung up as the railroad was being built. Redfield
was about 70 miles from James Martin's home in Branchville.
There was only 21 months between her marriage to Anson and
her marriage to John Sikes. Sarah would have her second child,
Robert Sikes, on 15 August 1886. She probably thought she was
finally going to find happiness. Unfortunately, more dark clouds
were on the horizon. Before his thirtieth birthday, her second
husband, John Sikes, died. Sarah was again a widow and this
time with two young children.

James Martin and Sarah

We are not sure how James Martin and Sarah found each
other. We know that before she married, she and her mother
were living in nearby Dallas County. When she married John
Sikes she lived in northwestern Jefferson County. We know the
courtship wasn't long. One day before Andrew Douglas's first
birthday (Mandy's last child) Sarah and James Martin were
married, Sarah's third marriage in only seven short years. Rev.
W. H. Hinton performed the ceremony on Wednesday, 20 June
1888, somewhere in Lincoln County. Almost certainly James
Martin's father Larkin attended the ceremony as well as most of
the tiny community of Branchville. A service in the middle of
the week could indicate this was not a big social event – but it
was not uncommon, either. Two people, both single heads of
households, with children, in a harsh environment; remarriage
was expected. Friends and neighbors probably began almost
immediately after the death of their spouses looking for possible
mates for them. That's just how things were. James Martin
brought eight children into the marriage and Sarah brought two.
Some might think a family with ten children would be close to
the limit, but time would prove that James Martin and Sarah
were comfortable with considerably more.

James Martin Leaves Branchville

The new family decided it was time to change their surroundings, a time for new beginnings, and perhaps a place Sarah could call hers, after living in "Mandy's house." Shortly after their marriage, James Martin and Sarah packed up the huge household and moved to Whiteville Township, about 18 miles up the road toward Pine Bluff. The trip would have been by mule-drawn wagons, traveling around two miles per hour. The family's belongings would have been in the wagon, with those able to walk plodding along beside. Very probably James Martin went on ahead and got things ready, and it is also possible that the mule-drawn wagon made several trips to their new home moving all the family's belongings. James's younger brother, John Nicholas, lived near their Branchville home, so he could have helped with the move and lessoned the number of trips. Also Larkin, his father, lived nearby. So we don't know for sure if the family moved in one trip using the wagons of relatives, or if they made several trips. What we do know is that eighteen months after their wedding was recorded back in Lincoln County (Branchville), James Martin was paying taxes in Jefferson County (Whiteville), his new home.

While Pine Bluff was the nearest town of any size, it was still more than eleven miles into town. Their Branchville home back in Lincoln County was only four and a half miles from the largest town and county seat, Star City. Pine Bluff in 1890 was a city of almost 10,000 with countless stores and far more supplies than were available in Star City – but the trip into Pine Bluff was over five hours away by wagon. To get back home before dark, they would have to leave at or before first light. Things were different here. Not worse, by any means, just different.

Pine Bluff was booming. Cotton and river commerce helped fuel the boom. Businesses were moving into the area. The railroad came to town in 1873, telephone service began in 1883. Soon James Martin and Sarah would own 160 acres of good land in Whiteville Township. Later, Larkin would purchase another 40 acres adjoining theirs, giving them a combined 200 acres to farm. Their new home and land was near where Harmony Missionary Baptist Church stands today. The land is fertile and covered with pine trees. By the time of the 1920 census, a network of roads had developed. The census records show they lived along "Middle Warren Road." Many roads still had no names and were referred to as "rural roads." Others just indicated people lived along a rural postal route. At this time, we have not been able to determine exactly where on the road they lived but maps show the approximate location and clearly show the road.

While Sarah and James Martin were married in June of 1888, their first child, Jennie Bell, would not be born until four years later in June of 1892. By this time James Martin's first son Calvin was already 19 and my grandfather, Charles Larkin, was seventeen. Albert was 15, William Claudis twelve, Thomas was eleven, and Thomas (Strait) from Sarah's first husband was ten. Mandy's last child Andrew, was five but probably spoiled rotten by his five older brothers and two older sisters as was probably also the case with young Robert (Sikes), age six, Sarah's second son by her second husband.

Sarah's Household—Lots of Change

Sarah and James Martin's first son, Edgar Austin, was born 11 January 1895. Another daughter, Bertha Leona, followed in 1898. Even as James Martin and Sarah were adding Jennie Bell, Austin, and Bertha to their roster of children, the older ones were starting to leave home. Calvin was in his mid- to late twenties, and Charlie and Albert in their mid-twenties. The 1900 census does not show Calvin in the home, and by that time

Charlie and Albert had already been making their fortune in Texas. The 1900 census does show Charlie and Albert as being in James Martin's household but this probably indicated they were "in and out," as Charlie had married Ada Stewart, in Bell County, Texas, on 13 August 1898, the same year Bertha Leona was born. We see evidence that Charlie's younger brother Albert was in Texas with him. Charlie and Ada had their first child, Claude Willis, in Bell County, on 7 June 1899. So they were definitely not under James Martin and Sarah's roof any longer. Sarah's first son, Thomas, was also not with her, but living back in Lincoln County with their previous Branchville neighbors. He would have been in his late teens and probably working back there.

Larkin Leaves Lincoln County

About this time James Martin's father, Larkin Harrison, may have decided his eighty acres was getting a bit too much for him to manage as his flock all left the nest. His sons had begun families of their own with farms of their own just as James Martin had. We don't know the exact date but toward the end of the 1890s Larkin sold his eighty acres in Branchville and joined his son in Whiteville Township, Jefferson County, Arkansas. He found a neighbor of James Martin's named George Hunt, who owned quite a bit of land in the area and had agreed to sell Larkin 40 acres adjoining the land of his son James Martin. According to the deed, Larkin paid George Hunt and his wife Ida $150 for the 40-acre parcel, which works out to $3.75 an acre. It's not known if this value is actual or a figure agreed upon to reduce taxes. As an interesting side note, James Martin's oldest daughter Cora was married to Henry Hunt and already had a family before 1900, so there is a high probability Henry was related to George Hunt. We're not sure who led the Jacks family exodus from Lincoln County but shortly after James

James Martin and Sarah With Their Children

Martin and Sarah arrived, the area around Whiteville Township
was significantly populated by the Jacks clan. Larkin was born
in 1826 so by this time he would have been in his early seven-
ties. Even though he owned the 40 acres adjoining his son's
land, in accordance with the custom of the time James Martin
and Sarah welcomed Larkin into their home. He lived with them
until his death a few years later in 1908.

Sarah and James Martin would continue having children.
After Bertha came Henry Floyd on 14 December 1900, May or
Mary born 5 May 1903, Fred Nicholas born 24 February 1906,
Arthur Garland on 14 October 1908, Ruby on 24 June 1911,
and finally Bessie Ione in June of 1915. From the time of her
marriage to James Martin in 1888 until the birth of her last
child, Sarah Lucinda would give James Martin nine children.
Altogether, counting Thomas Albert and Robert from her first
and second husbands, Sarah would have eleven children. Sarah
gave birth to her first child when she was sixteen and her last
when she was forty-nine. James Martin was almost sixty-three
when their last child was born.

Harmony Missionary Baptist Church

Sarah and James Martin were active in church. In 1899
Harmony Missionary Baptist Church was founded and early
church records show Mr. and Mrs. J. M. Jacks as two of the 13
charter members. The church was the center of the community.
Several Jacks family members would meet their spouses at
Harmony's services. Long after J. M. and Sarah had passed away,
a substantial number of the church's congregation were sons and
daughters, grandchildren, or even great-grandchildren of J. M.
and Sarah. Even today their descendents continue to attend
Harmony Missionary Baptist Church, the church of their ancestors. And when their life on this earth is finished, they will be
buried there, just behind the church, near J. M. and Sarah.

A Changing World

James Martin and Sarah would begin to witness a more rapidly paced world as the century turned. Two brothers who owned a successful bicycle shop designed and actually flew a "flying machine." Three years later in 1906 about 75% of San Francisco's residents found themselves homeless due to an enormous earthquake and resultant fire. The government was saying only about 500 people died but reports were coming out of the area saying probably close to 3,000 were actually dead and many suspected the government was intentionally reporting lesser numbers, for fear the truth would thwart expansion of the area. New York City would open a public transportation system that ran underground. It was called a "subway." In far away Russia, bloody social unrest was taking place. Just next to them, the territory of Oklahoma became a state. Two years after the earthquake, a man named Ford would design an "automobile." He called it the Model T. These Model T automobiles would soon be in Pine Bluff. The "Indian Head" penny they all used daily was replaced with one bearing the image of Abraham Lincoln. Grandchildren were being born at exponential rates. And the lure of Texas was calling many more of the Jacks clan. Life around James Martin and Sarah was accelerating.

"The Old Generation Will Pass Away but a New Will Come to Take Its Place"

Larkin Harrison Jacks died peacefully in the home of his son James Martin on Friday, 24 July 1908. He was 83. He was born in 1826 and witnessed astounding changes . . . a machine that enabled men to fly, the automobile, a device that allowed the human voice to travel down a wire for hundreds of miles making long-distance conversations possible. He had to leave his home and family and fight in a war that took the lives of hundreds of thousands . . . Americans fighting Americans. In many ways this was a wise man whose influence on his children and grandchildren must have been profound. James and Sarah would bury their son Thomas, who died on 28 December 1910 at the age of 27, in the cemetery behind Harmony Missionary Baptist Church. Thomas was probably the first of the Jacks family to be buried there. Many would follow.

Late on the night of Wednesday, 2 September 1914, or early Thursday morning, word would come to James Martin that his second son, Charles Larkin (Charlie), now living in Texas, had been shot and was in very serious condition. His third son Albert was there with him. The family came together as they always did. For days, Charlie would cling to life, but finally the raging infections caused by the two bullets that ripped into his body – one penetrating his left lung – would overcome him. James Martin's son, Charles Larkin Jacks, died on the afternoon of Friday, 11 September 1914, surrounded by his wife and children. He was buried in the North Belton Cemetery. Charlie was the first of numerous descendents of James Martin to be buried in their new home, Texas.

The Last Years

The last years of James Martin and Sarah were, by most standards, blessed. They were active in the Harmony Missionary Baptist Church; their children and grandchildren lived all around them. They were respected in the community. They lived through World War I . . . a war in which nearly 9 million people lost their lives and about 22 million more were wounded. Their sons registered for the draft. From their draft registration cards we learned that sons Albert, William Claudis, and Andrew all had gray or blue eyes and black or dark hair. All the children of Charlie Jacks had dark hair and gray-blue eyes. We learned that Albert was living in Llano, Llano County, Texas, in 1918 (apparently he left Bell County after his brother Charlie was murdered). His profession was listed as merchant. His younger brothers William and Andrew elected to stay behind in Jefferson County, near the area where their father lived. Their address was RFD (rural free delivery) Route #2 and they lived close to each other. William was Box 265 and Andrew was Box 267, both on the outskirts of Pine Bluff near the Whiteville community.

James Martin Dies

On Saturday, 7 July 1923, James Martin Jacks passed away in his home. Since most of his family was nearby, the funeral was held the following day. By today's customs, the funeral would have been unusual but in light of many things, it was very understandable; unusual in that it was held on Sunday morning at 10:00. This would have been normal church time. But since this was a charter member of the church, and a significant number of the church's congregation were his direct descendents or relatives, the funeral itself being the Sunday morning service was quite understandable. No doubt the pastor, Rev. Mr. Kelly, used the opportunity to invite anyone who did not know the Lord to speak with him after the service. At the conclusion of the service, the casket would have been taken only a few yards away into the cemetery behind the church. Today, his grave marker stands in a prominent location in the cemetery, and today, a significant number of the graves in Harmony Missionary Baptist Church's cemetery are Jacks family graves. As a footnote, the date of his death as inscribed on his tombstone appears to be incorrect. The date on the stone as well as the date in numerous genealogy records is shown as 8 July 1923. We believe he died on the 7th and was buried on the 8th. Years later, when the new stone was being erected they probably mistakenly took the date of his funeral service rather than the date of his actual death.

In addition, the year of his birth, as inscribed on the tomb-

James Martin Jacks

stone also appears to be incorrect. Our family records, including inscriptions on the back of an old picture as well as the 1900 U. S, Census read 1852 as the year of his birth, while his grave marker reads 1850. The obituary below which appeared in the *Pine Bluff Commercial* on Monday, July 9, 1923, reads:

"J.M. Jacks . . . The funeral of J.M. Jacks, 71, well known farmer of this city, who died Saturday morning at his home 12 miles south of Pine Bluff was conducted at 10 o'clock Sunday morning at Harmony Church, Rev. Mr. Kelly officiating. Mr. Jacks had been a resident of Jefferson county most of his life and as a member of Harmony Church for 50 years. He is survived by his widow and 15 children. They are J.V. Jacks of Grand Okla., A.L. Jacks of Strep Springs, Tex., E.A. Jacks of Grimshad, Tex., W.C., A.D., H.F., and Arthur Jacks of Pine Bluff. Mrs. J.L. Hankins of Brownsville, Tex., Mrs. H.C. Hunt, Mrs. W.H. Tucker, Mrs. A.E. Harris, Mrs. Z.T. Stone, Miss Ruby Jacks and Miss Ione Jacks all of Pine Bluff. A large number of grandchildren also survive."

It is not uncommon for such articles to contain errors. The ones detected thus far are: J. M. was probably a member of Harmony Missionary Baptist Church for more like 25 years than fifty. The church was chartered in 1899. J. M. died in 1923 and he moved to Jefferson County from Mill Creek in Lincoln County after June 1888 and before December 31 1890. "J. V." Jacks is most likely Calvin James Jacks, as he is the only one whom we can find with connections to Oklahoma. Considering some close family member had to assemble all this information and rush it to the newspaper in Pine Bluff, probably written out by hand, mistakes would be expected. It should be noted here that the family by stating his age as 71 is confirming the birth year as 1852. Also of interest, the two unmarried daughters mentioned in the obituary; Ruby and Ione, were ages twelve and eight respectively. Sarah, at age 57, was now a widow for the third time. This time she would not remarry, and would live the rest of her life there just outside Pine Bluff surrounded by her children, step-children and innumerable grandchildren.

Sarah's Last Years

The 1930 U.S. Census tells us a lot about Sarah's last years. Another child would die; her daughter May. May had married W. Zack Stone, but on 10 October 1926, she died leaving a son, Zack Stone. Sarah would, like so many times before, exercise her maternal nature. The 1930 Census shows Sarah as head of household, raising eight-year-old Zack. The same census also shows people believed to be Zack's paternal grandparents living nearby. They also attended Harmony Missionary Baptist Church. Probably young Zack spent plenty of time with both families.

In addition, a study of the 1900, 1920, and 1930 U.S. Census for Whiteville Township reveals a substantial number of the Jacks family households within the boundaries of this small sub-county political entity. Not only were they within the township . . . they were close . . . often living next to each other. Sarah had managed in her last years, most probably due to her loving character, to surround herself with what was so lacking in her early life . . . enduring love, happiness, and security.

Sarah Lucinda Jacks died on Sunday morning, 16 March, 1941, in her home. She had lived 75 years. Her life been full. Her obituary in the *Pine Bluff Graphic* for Monday, 17 March edition reads: "FUNERAL SERVICES THIS AFTERNOON FOR MRS. JACKS

"Mrs. Sarah Jacks, 75, wife of the late J. M. Jacks, died Sunday morning at 11:15 o'clock at her home in the

Harmony Community, following a short illness. She was born in Jefferson County January 21 1866, and had lived in this county all her life and had made her home in the Harmony Community for the past 50 years. She was a devoted wife and mother and was loved by all who knew her. Mrs. Jacks is survived by seven sons, T.A. Strait of Houston, Texas, R.S. Sikes of Pine Bluff, Andy Jacks, Floyd Jacks, and Fred Jacks of Pine Bluff, Edgar Jacks and Arthur Jacks of Houston, Texas, four daughters, Mrs. J.B. Ballew and Mrs. Arthur Harris of Pine Bluff, Mrs. Otho McBurnett of Altheimer, Mrs. Grady Edwards of Little Rock, two stepsons, W.C. Jacks of Pine Bluff and Albert Jacks of Gorman Texas; one stepdaughter, Mrs. J.L. Hankins of Abilene, Texas; 34 grandchildren; 21 great grandchildren, and numbers of other relatives. Funeral services were held at 3:30 o'clock this afternoon from the Harmony Baptist Church in charge of the Rev. F.A. Courtney, pastor of the Harmony Baptist Church and the Rev. H.S. McLaren, pastor of the Oakland Baptist Church at Hot Springs. Burial was on the family lot in Harmony Cemetery in charge of Ralph Robinson and Son Mortuary. Active pallbearers were J.H. Blundell, Carmell McMillan, Calvin McMillan, Virgil Reed and Jessie Gentry. Honorary pallbearers were H.H. Mundell, W.M. Edwards, Oscar Smith, C.M. Ross, C.A. Newton, R.A. Barnes, E.M. Rucker, Melvin Grimes, Ed Glover, J.T. Palmer, Dr. Virgil Payne, and W.A. Owen."

CHAPTER 9

CHARLES LARKIN "CHARLIE" JACKS

6 February 1875 – 11 September 1914

One of Seventeen Children

My father's father was Charles Larkin Jacks but everybody called him Charlie. He was born in a little place called Branchville in Mill Creek Township in what is now Lincoln County, Arkansas, on a cold Saturday morning, February 6, 1875. He was the second child born to James Martin and Amanda L. "Manda" or "Mandy" Bailey. Charlie grew up knowing about large families. His father and his mother Amanda would have seven children. But Amanda died in 1889 when Charlie was only fourteen, and his father then married a twice-widowed lady named Sarah Lucinda Wortham. She brought two children into the marriage, and then Sarah and James Martin had nine more. So in reality Charlie was the second of his father's seventeen children. In the early years of James Martin and Amanda's marriage they shared a home with her mother and father. At this time, her family, the Baileys, still had three children living at home. Later, Charlie would have the opportunity to live with another grandfather, his father's father, Larkin Harrison Jacks, who would come to live out the last years of his life with them.

A Vanishing Dimension

At first glance, this sounds like an almost unbearable circumstance in which to grow up but in reality it was more the norm than not. Couples often lived with parents during the first years of their marriage and older parents often came to live with children in their last years. Rather than being a hardship, it increased family bonds.

Branchville ... A Dirt Poor Hard Life

If you had to pick one word to describe Branchville in the 1870s, it would be poverty; poor farmers trying to scratch out a living from their small parcels of land, surrounded by the tall pine trees. It was a time when a laborer might only earn fifty cents a day – on a good day, a dollar. To deepen the hard economic times, now scores of freed illiterate slaves were trying to find work in a market that didn't offer much work. Their plight was even worse. And to deepen the severity of the economic conditions, the policies of Reconstruction were doing anything but reconstructing. All this would have a much harsher impact on Charlie's father James Martin, but without doubt it would also have an influence on Charlie's character.

Sickness and disease killed many; malaria, yellow fever, also known as "yellow jack," and pneumonia were just some of the life-claiming illnesses Charlie's family had to face. They had only primitive medicines like "turpentine emulsion" and quinine pills. They lived in a world in which antibiotics did not yet exist. These conditions killed family, kin, and acquaintances. Infant mortality was high; many of the graves in the Branchville area from that era are those of infants.

Charlie's Mother Dies

Charlie would learn firsthand about the sorrow of death. When he was fourteen, his mother died shortly after the birth of her eighth child, Andrew. She was only 35. She was buried just down the road from where they lived, in a small cemetery on land donated by the Norton family. The year was 1887. There were no automobiles. It is doubtful there was a mortician. She probably was buried within 24 hours of her death and her body either transported down the road by wagon or the casket carried down the road by male members of the church. Her grave has been lost to time, her grave marker is no longer visible.

Sharing a small log or plank board cabin with eight mother-less children and a widowed father, struggling to scratch out a living in this harsh environment, must have held numerous joyless hours for young Charlie. The following year, Charlie's father would understandably take another wife; this was the way things worked. She was only 22 years of age, and already widowed twice with two children. With this second wife, Charlie's father would have nine more children in addition to the two sons she already had. As a matter of fact, Charlie's father would have his seventeenth and last child a year after Charlie died in 1914.

Crops and Meals

Charlie and his siblings all had to work on their land so the family could survive. They planted vegetables to preserve for food in the winter. They planted melons, squash, potatoes, sweet potatoes, onions, garlic, and other vegetables for food during the spring, summer, and fall. The potatoes and onions and other root vegetables would go in storage for the winter. Corn was not only for them but also helped feed their animals. It was cheaper to grind your corn into corn flour and corn meal than to buy wheat flour at the store down the road. All of this meant Charlie and his brothers and sisters would spend hours in the hot fields tending to these crops.

Chickens provided meat and eggs. Pigs were cured in the

smokehouse for meat during the winter. Butchering these hogs was hard work too, and took several of the family an entire day. A few cows would provide milk, cream, butter, and more meat. Not much was left unused. Charlie's father would tan the pig and cow hides and the leather would be used; chair seats, belts, harnesses, straps and thongs – they tried to use it all. Water came from springs and wells. It had to be hauled to the house in water barrels. This too was hard work. Wild grapes and plums as well as planted fruit trees (peaches, apples, and plums) provided Charlie's family with fresh fruit in the summer and more food to preserve for the winter. The mustang grapes were everywhere, grew wild, required no care, and made great jelly and jam – if sweetened with enough sugar. It is not known if Charlie's father made mustang grape wine but it certainly was a common practice.

When Charlie was growing up, a store-bought hunting rifle could easily cost a month's pay. While we don't know for sure, they probably used an old Civil War surplus, single-shot, muzzle-loading, black powder-type gun that used a percussion cap firing mechanism and fired a ball or minie-ball bullet. But, like most of their other poor neighbors, they relied heavily on trapping possums, coons, rabbits, porcupines, and squirrels. Because this wild meat contained little fat, it was tough and therefore usually eaten in stews. They would have eaten them in dumpling stews also. Catfish and crawfish also helped feed the family. The crawfish had a somewhat muddy taste, but were easy to catch (a string with pork fat tied to the end) and could be done by the younger children.

But all this hard work produced many good things; fresh hot cornbread, cornpone, sweet potatoes cooked in Dutch ovens, Irish potatoes cooked by being buried in hot ashes in the fireplace in winter or in the outside cooking area in the summer. Iron pots full of vegetable and beef stew would simmer over the coals. Breakfasts of salt-pork, eggs, and cornpone gave them the energy to work till the noon meal called "dinner." Dinner was the main meal of the day. It gave the nourishment needed to continue in the field or other tasks until daylight was almost gone. On special occasions like Sunday dinner, hot, fluffy biscuits made from store-bought flour adorned fried chicken, boiled eggs, and fresh vegetables if it was summer. The evening meal called "supper" was a lighter meal than dinner. Over time this would slowly change and "supper" would become the main meal. As a matter of fact, by the time Charlie was running his own restaurant in Texas, "supper" had become the day's primary meal.

Family Transportation

Mules pulled heavily loaded wagons down deeply rutted roads which became virtually impassable when it rained. While they lived just down the road from the store and post office, rains frequently made these roads difficult to travel. If you needed to take some of your pine trees to the saw mill, you had to wait till the heavy wagons could pass without getting stuck. Many who didn't wait long enough found themselves unloading their heavy cargo beside the road and waiting for others to come along to help free the wagon. For sure Charlie knew how to handle a wagon and a team of mules.

Charlie's Early Schooling

Schools were vastly different in Charlie's day. Historical records from the mid-1870s show that while the county had 1618 white children and 2018 "colored" children, for a total of 3636, only 1109 white children and 1244 black children were enrolled in school; 68% and 62% respectively. The value of an education, at least a fundamental comprehension of the "3 Rs" was probably well understood by the parents. But children were an essential part of a family's workforce if the family was to extract even the most basic level of subsistence from their land. Records indicate that in 1891 still more than 25% of the state's residents could not read and write. We can find no accurate record of Charlie's education but from the U. S. Census records, we know Charlie attended school and was able to read and write. Later we see he could do both well enough to own a confectionary business in Haskell and a restaurant business in Belton.

Charlie Leaves Arkansas

Although by the mid 1890s Charlie's father and family were managing fairly well, Charlie struck out for Texas in search of a brighter future. We can't be sure but he almost certainly traveled to Belton mostly or entirely by train. The rail system had been well-developed in that part of Texas by then. We can't find a record of the exact date when he arrived in Bell County, but we know by the summer of 1898 he had been there long enough to meet and fall in love with a beautiful young lady from Tennessee Valley in northwestern Bell County.

Belton and Bell County

The Belton of the late 1890s was right out of a novel. It was a booming frontier county seat town. Fist fights, gun fights, the railroad, vigilante justice, Texas Rangers, outlaws, the Chisholm Trail, saloons, and until recently, Indians . . . Belton had it all.

Charlie Meets Ada Stewart

Soon after arriving in Bell County, Charlie met a beautiful young lady named Ada D. Stewart. Ada was born in Pulaski, Giles County, Tennessee, on 29 October 1879. While her family was part of the famous "Scotch-Irish" group, they had been in America since before the Revolution and her 2nd great-grandfa-

Charles Larkin Jacks

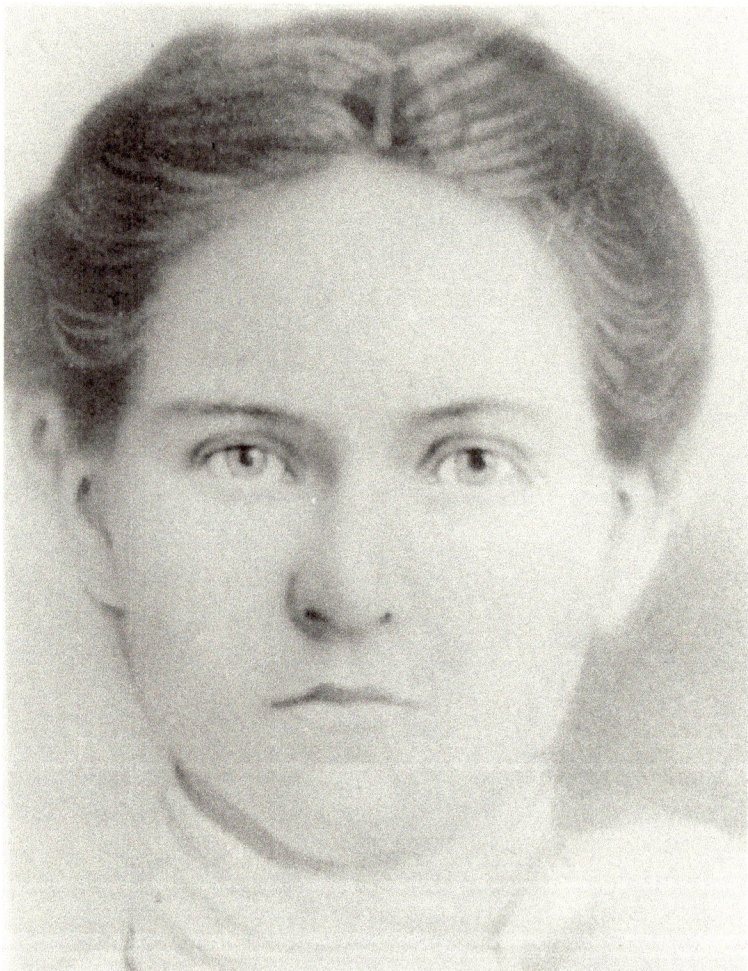

Ada Stewart Jacks

ther, John Stewart, born in County Down, Ireland, had been a patriot who fought in the Revolutionary War.

Ada arrived in Bell County with her extended family clan by train from Tennessee in 1882, when she was about two years old. They settled in an area known as Tennessee Valley located on the banks of the Leon River. It was a beautiful fertile area of hills and valleys (now all under Lake Belton). Charlie married Ada D. Stewart on Saturday, 13 August 1898. Charlie was 23 and Ada was almost 19. It was a beautiful day for a wedding with the temperature only 92 degrees. That was one of the coolest days Bell County would see that month. The ladies at the wedding were certainly fanning themselves briskly in an attempt to provide some relief from the 92 degree blessing they had received. Ten months after they were married, their first child was born. Charlie and Ada named him Claude Willis. While we do not know for certain, Charlie had a younger brother named William Claudis, and Claude was probably named for him.

Charlie and Ada first made their home in a little community called Summer's Mill located on Salado Creek, five miles southeast of Belton. In 1896 the little community had seventy-five residents, a general store, a flour mill and a saw mill, and, of course, a cotton gin. The farms in the area raised cotton and wheat. Since they were not landowners at that time, Charlie must have been employed in one of the local businesses or worked on one of the many farms. Bell County was booming then the railroads were bringing people and business activity to the area. The Missouri, Kansas and Texas Railroad, also known as the Katy, went through Belton. Jobs were plentiful and so were opportunities. Charlie was raised on a farm but it is interesting to note he chose not to follow that way of life in Texas.

Albert Joins Charlie in Texas

It was about this time that Charlie's younger brother Albert left Pine Bluff, and joined Charlie in Texas. He settled in Belton about five miles from Summer's Mill. Soon Albert would go into the restaurant business. It's not known who got in that business first, but both would operate restaurants in the Belton-Temple area. Albert ran restaurants or cafes in both Belton and Temple. We only have record of Charlie being in that business in Belton.

Far away from sleepy Summer's Mill, history was moving forward at an amazing pace. Spain and the United States fought a ten-week war which would see the United States emerge victorious, gaining control of Cuba, Puerto Rico, Guam, and the Philippines. Another, more subtle result of the war, was played out on the pages of the American presses. The public saw whites and blacks, northerners and southerners, all fighting side by side in a "victorious and noble cause." The country needed this healing. This Spanish-American conflict also introduced Theodore Roosevelt to the world stage. While history refers to the period from the end of Reconstruction (1876) to the turn of the century as The Gilded Age, little of this glittering wealth was visible to most of Texas's rural populations. It was nevertheless a prosperous period for Texans in general. The population of Texas grew rapidly from 1,591,749 in 1880 to 2,235,527 by 1890 and reached 3,048,710 in 1900. By contrast, Arkansas' 1900 population was 1,311,564. Texas was receiving a steady flow of immigrants from other states, primarily the southern states. In addition there was a large influx of German immigrants around this time. All these people meant economic growth and opportunities. The majority of Texans still lived and worked in rural areas. In 1880 this number was 90.8 percent. By 1900 the figure had dropped slightly to 82.9 percent. Charlie and Ada would be part of this drop. Sometime shortly after the birth of their second child on 24 August 1901 – this time a girl named Una Lee – they left Summer's Mill and moved five miles away to Belton. The move was almost certainly an attempt to become part of the growing prosperity associated with the rapid influx of people coming into Texas. While we don't know for certain, Charlie probably began his restaurant and cafe career with the move.

While living in Belton, their third child, another daughter, was born. Her name was Ruth Nolan. She was born on 12 February 1906. Sometime in 1906, after Ruth's birth, the family left Belton and moved to Haskell, in Haskell County, Texas. Haskell was a small town in the Rolling Plains region of Northwest Texas. This was a move of almost 250 miles and would have been a significant journey for the young family. Since Henry Ford did not introduce his Model T until 1908, most probably the family made the journey by rail.

Haskell – Texas Boomtown

In 1880 Haskell County had 48 residents and two ranches. By 1890 the county had 1665 residents and 105 ranches. In 1900, the census reported 256 farms and ranches and 2637 residents. In twenty short years the county's population had gone from 48 to 2637. In 1900 the county had no railroad service. By 1908 two railway companies served Haskell County. Without doubt Charlie had heard about this population explosion and hoped to be in on the ground floor of all the opportunities that came with such growth. The 1910 census recorded a population explosion with 2210 farms and 16,249 residents. This growth was taking place in other counties in the area as well, as cotton farming and railways arrived.

In addition to being cattle country, Haskell County also had farmland. In 1890 the county had 1421 acres planted in corn and 1340 in cotton. Amazing agricultural growth statistics were reported again in 1900 and 1910. The 1910 figures reported

18,420 acres under cultivation in corn, 1,893 in wheat, and more than 75,000 acres in cotton. But fate would not continue to smile for long on this boomtown mentality. Not too long after Charlie and his family arrived in Haskell the economy started to slow down; while not as devastating as the dust bowl era that would hit in the 1930s, this downturn was significant for the newly arrived and not yet firmly established Jacks family.

We see from the 1910 census that Charlie and Ada owned their own home in Haskell but that it had a mortgage. The census also showed that Charlie was in the "confection" business. It is a bit difficult to tell what was meant by the word "confection" at the turn of the century as the American English language use of the word today shows some variance with the European English language use, but generally it would have referred to a wide range of candies. It is not known if Charlie made candy or if he only had a retail store. Since he already had restaurant experience, he could have been making the confections.

James Martin Jacks Is Born

It was in Haskell on 10 October 1909 that my father, James Martin, was born. James was their second son and fourth child. James was soon known by his nickname Jimmie, a name that would be with him the rest of his life. Sunday, 10 October 1909 was a beautiful day. There was no rain; the high temperature was 81 degrees, the low temperature 41 degrees. We don't know if James Martin was born in a hospital or at home but we have a wrist ID made from beads, such as were like the ones used in hospital nurseries, with his name laced in the beads so we tend to believe that James Martin was the first of their children to be born in a hospital. He was also the first of Charlie and Ada's children to have a birth certificate. His older brother and two sisters would apply for theirs decades later.

The Family Returns to Belton

We don't know for sure when they arrived in Haskell and we don't know exactly when they decided to "go back home" to Bell County but go they did. The economic downturn Haskell was experiencing made Charlie and Ada's young family one of the statistics in the records of the significant exodus. Haskell County lost 12.6% of its population between 1910 and 1920. The family of Charles Larkin and Ada D. Jacks was part of that 12.6%. They had friends and family in Bell County, they were young and energetic, they would start over. Soon after their arrival, Charlie went back into the restaurant business. His brother Albert had a cafe in Temple about 12 miles north of Belton on the road to Waco. We're not sure how the brothers transitioned from the farm-based lives they knew back in Arkansas to the cafe and restaurant business, but their motivation would not be hard to understand. Scratching out a living in that Arkansas dirt in 100-degree heat couldn't have held a lot of attraction for either of them.

Life in Belton

Soon after returning, Charlie secured a location for his cafe at 130 S. East Street and opened his new business. The address is still a valid address today, just across the street from the Bell County Courthouse. It was bounded on one side by Central Avenue and on the other by Water Street. While this was a central location, it was not without drawbacks.

Back then, eating establishments were more "cafes" than restaurants. There were tables of course, but a mainstay of the establishment was the "counter." Businessmen left their shops to have lunch there as well as those who worked in the courthouse or found themselves nearby on business about lunchtime. These counters were the social centers of the business community. Around midmorning many of the town's business owners would walk over to the cafe and sit at the counter for a cup of coffee and some conversation. In the evenings, the workers who were in town for the many construction projects ate in these downtown cafes. There were several saloons in the area also. This didn't do a lot to help the East Street's reputation. The streets were mud and mule-drawn wagons were common. Tracks ran through the unpaved streets where "street cars" moved slowly. Most of the buildings in the area were constructed from locally-quarried limestone and were one- or two-story structures. They were almost all long, narrow, and rectangular in shape, with narrow fronts to accommodate more establishments along the street frontage.

Charlie and Ada found a house to rent just a few blocks from the cafe. It was a nice wood-frame house, of medium size for the time, with a large front porch and shaded yard for the children to play in. Each day Charlie would make the approximately ten-minute walk to and from work. While it must have been a pleasant stroll most of the time, the winter walks probably were less than enjoyable. Belton, while enjoying growth and modernization, was still at times very much a wild-west town. Fights were common and sometimes "justice" didn't wait for the court system. In 1910 a "vigilante" mob shot and killed a man suspected of killing a local constable, dragged his body around the square behind a wagon, and then burned it down to ashes next to the courthouse flagpole. Belton's last public hanging took place on Good Friday 1922.

Charles Larkin Jacks—The Gunfight

It reads like something straight out of the movies, but it's not; it happened to my grandfather, Charles Larkin Jacks.

Understanding completely the events that eventually claimed the life of Charlie Jacks in Belton, Texas, back in September of 1914 is now not possible. They have been ravaged by time to the point they will forever remain partially obscured to us. Nevertheless, by combining family legends with the research of two local Belton historians and old court records we've managed to pierce the veil of time and see – though as through a mist – what happened on that Wednesday evening, September 2, around 8:00 p.m. in Charlie Jacks' restaurant on the east side of Belton's square. Charlie's restaurant was on the less than sunny east side of Belton's square. A third historian – now in her nineties, who has worked at the local newspaper since she was thirteen – said that side of Belton's square back then was referred to as "rat row . . . because all the ladies of the evening would hang out there and men would go over there to drink and socialize." From old surveys and photos of the period, we know that at the time of Charlie's restaurant, the east side of the square had eight business establishments; three were saloons, one of which was also a pool hall, two other pool halls, and two restaurants. The streets of Belton at the time were unpaved. Dusty when dry . . . muddy when wet. Wagons pulled by horses and mules filled the streets. Many disagreements of the time were settled with fists or a gun.

Family tradition always said the problem between my grandfather and the man who killed him stemmed from the man's saloon next door. Charlie Jacks was shot and killed by a man named James (Jim or "Squab") Miller. Miller owned the saloon adjacent to my grandfather's restaurant. Legend has it that the patrons of the saloon did not like to be seen entering the saloon. They would enter Charlie Jacks' restaurant, walk all the way through the dining room, through the kitchen, and out the back door into the alley, and then enter the saloon via its back door . . . . thus avoiding the public's critical eye.

My aunts told me that the saloon's drunken patrons would disturb Charlie's restaurant diners as they passed through. They said that their father, on numerous occasions, had asked Jim

Miller to keep his back door closed and his customers out of the restaurant. Obviously this didn't happen and around 8 o'clock on the night of Wednesday, September 2, 1914 Squab Miller and Charlie Jacks faced off in Charlie's restaurant. Jacks family tradition said Miller was armed with a pistol and Charlie had a shotgun. Again, legend says – and at this time it appears we will never know all the details – that Charlie's shotgun misfired and he was struck by bullets from Miller's pistol. The portion of the Belton weekly newspaper's archives which carried the story were destroyed by fire many years ago. The Temple daily paper reported the shooting and gave regular updates of Charlie's condition. Here are the snippets from the *Temple Daily Telegraph* beginning immediately after the shooting.

> 3 September 1914 *Temple Daily Telegraph*: "PISTOL DUEL LAST NIGHT ---- Two Belton Citizens Shower Down on Each Other --- One Is Hit. Belton, Sept 2 --- In a gun fight in the Jacks restaurant on the east side of the square at 8 o'clock tonight between Jim Miller and Charles Jacks, the latter was wounded in the shoulder and arm, the seriousness of which is not known at this time. Four or five shots were exchanged during the scrap and much excitement in that section prevailed for a time. Disagreement over business matters was given as the cause of the trouble."

> 4 September *Temple Daily Telegraph*: "Miller Under Bond ---- Belton Sept 3 --- Jim Miller, under arrest for shooting 'Albert Jacks' [this is incorrect and should read Charlie Jacks . . . Albert was Charlie's brother and lived in Temple] when these two men engaged in a gun fight in the latter's place of business last night was placed under $500 bond today.

Mr. Jacks, who received two pistol wounds, one in the arm and one in the shoulder, is still suffering considerably, his condition is reported as being unchanged late tonight."

5 September *Temple Daily Telegraph*: "Charley Jacks' Condition Serious.
Belton, Sept. 4. ---- Charley Jacks who was wounded Wednesday night in a difficulty which occurred in his restaurant is reported as not resting well today. It is thought his condition is growing more serious. The bullet which entered just in front of the left shoulder penetrated the upper part of the lung."

9 September *Temple Daily Telegraph*: "Condition of Charley Jacks.
Belton, Sept. 8 ---- Charley Jacks is reported as having rested very nicely this morning but as not being so well this afternoon."

11 September *Temple Daily Telegraph*: "Charley Jacks Worse.
Belton, Sept. 10 ---- The condition of Charley Jacks is reported critical this evening."

2 September *Temple Daily Telegraph*: "Bond Fixed at $10,000.
Belton, Sept. 11 ---- Following the death of Charley Jacks which occurred at 6:00 pm this afternoon, Jim Miller was placed under arrest charged with murder. It is charged that Jacks' death resulted from wounds received in an encounter with Miller several days ago. Miller was granted bond in the sum of $10,000."

Charlie's Death
Charlie Jacks died before he reached his 40th birthday. As

evidenced from the news clips, his passing was slow and painful, almost certainly due to an infection. There were no antibiotics at that time. He lay in his bed, visited daily by his doctor, surrounded by his family, and slowly slipped away. With nothing but electric fans and damp cloths, his family could do little to shield him from the temperatures which reached the low 90s each day. While the nights brought some relief with temperatures in the low 70s, the family was helpless to defend him from the fever that raged inside him. Newspaper reports say he was in great pain, so probably his doctor was using morphine in an attempt to help him rest, hoping his body might be able to fight off the infection. From Wednesday evening, 2 September, when the two bullets fired by Squab Miller entered his body, Charlie desperately clung to life. For nine pain-filled days Charlie fought to stay alive. But fighting the raging infection required strength and with each day Charlie used more and more of his reserve. Finally he could fight no more and he surrendered to death's call. Friday, 11 September 1914, around 6:00 p.m., Charles Larkin Jacks died in the bed he and Ada had shared. It was just before sunset. He left his widow Ada D. Stewart Jacks (age 35) and four children, Claude Willis Jacks, 15, Una Lee Jacks, 13, Ruth Nolan Jacks, 8, and James Martin Jacks, not quite 5. They buried Charlie in the cemetery on the north side of town now know as North Belton Cemetery. Charlie Jacks and his wife Ada (who never remarried) are buried side by side, along with his oldest son Claude Willis Jacks and his wife Viola. They're buried in plot number 457.

Charlie's son, Claude Willis Jacks, at age fifteen became the immediate de facto head of the family, taking on all the responsibilities previously borne by his father. As such, he operated a successful restaurant in Belton for over fifty years. Claude was an institution in the restaurant business in Belton. He became the success Charlie had hoped to become. Claude operated the

Avenue Cafe in the heart of Belton for decades. He was famous for his ever-present White Owl cigar and beaming smile.

The death of their father left an indelible mark on all his children. The event was so traumatic for young James Martin that he disliked talking about the event and I can only recall him doing it once. The conversation, a result of my question about how my grandfather died, lasted less than thirty seconds. All firsthand information I ever had about Charlie Jacks' death came from my Aunt Ruth.

Jim (Squab) Miller Footnote

Meanwhile, after several delays, Jim Miller finally stood trial for murder on 15 February 1917. With the help of a good attorney, he agreed to plead guilty and under the provisions of a relatively new law passed in 1911, he received a two- to five-year sentence which was suspended for good behavior. Therefore Jim Miller never served any prison time for the murder. With the help of two excellent Belton historians, we secured copies of all the court proceedings and were able to view the attorney's strategy as it unfolded. Unfortunately, the sheriff's records could not be located.

Court records indicate that Jim Miller was indicted on a charge of murder by a grand jury on 12 November 1914 ("with his malice and forethought kill and murder Chas Jacks by [unreadable word] and there shooting him, the said Chas Jacks with a pistol"). When the case finally came to trial in January of 1917, the charge had been reduced from murder to "manslaughter." In a prearranged agreement, Jim Miller pleaded guilty to the lesser charge and by the same prearranged agreement, received a sentence of "not less than two and not more than five years in prison." Then invoking the new Texas law enacted in 1911, Miller's attorneys got the two- to five- sentence suspended. The judge's instructions to the jury contained two options, one to send him to prison and the other which read as follows: "We the jury, find the defendant guilty as charged in the indictment, and assess his punishment at confinement for ____ years in the penitentiary, and we further find that the defendant has never before been convicted of a felony in this state or in any other state, and we recommend a suspension of sentence." The jury chose the suspended option on 15 February 1917. Jim Miller walked from that courtroom a free man without ever having served a minute in jail for the murder of Charlie Jacks.

In 1932 Jim Miller went back to that same District Court in Bell County and requested a new trial and that if a new trial was granted, the cause be dismissed. This is the judge's decision: ". . . it is accordingly considered, ordered, and adjudged by the court that the judgment of conviction heretofore rendered herein on the 15th day of February 1917, assessing his punishment at confinement in the penitentiary for a period of five years but with the sentence thereon suspended to and the same is hereby set aside, and a new trial granted herein, and this cause is hereby dismissed" . . . Jess Brewster, Judge 27th Judicial District.

So fifteen years after his conviction for killing Charlie Jacks, that conviction was "set aside" and the cause dismissed. One can't help but wonder what Ada thought about this. Perhaps she had forgiven Jim Miller years ago . . . and perhaps she hadn't. Just one more piece of the puzzle lost to time.

Ada Stewart Jacks Dies

Ada Jacks would live out the rest of her life under the care of her first son, Claude. When Claude purchased his home, he purchased the house next door for his mother. They lived side by side until her death. Ada Jacks died at age 55 in her home at 9:30 a.m. on Monday, 1 April 1935. She was surrounded by her family. Ada was buried beside her husband Charlie in North

Belton Cemetery. Ruth Jacks Brocker, Charlie and Ada's daughter, never moved from the Temple-Belton area. Almost daily she would visit their gravesite. She always kept it in perfect condition. Most of my knowledge of Charlie and Ada came from my Aunt Ruth.

Our First Generation of Texans

Charlie and Ada began our line of the Jacks family in Texas. Ada came to Bell County, Texas, from Tennessee in 1882 at the age of two. Charlie arrived in Bell County from Arkansas in the mid- to late 1890s; from these two pioneers have arisen to date (2010), four generations born in our beloved State of Texas.

CHAPTER 10

MY FATHER, JAMES MARTIN JACKS

10 October 1909 – 10 October 1976

Although I don't recall ever telling him, my father was my hero. With each passing year I continue to find more reasons for this. In so many ways, he was bigger than life. I regret never telling him. James Martin "Jimmie" Jacks was the fourth surviving child and second son born to Charles Larkin and Ada Stewart Jacks. He was the only one of their children not born in Bell County. Charlie and Ada had two other children, both girls, born before my father but who died in infancy. My father grew up as the baby of the family and by all accounts, "spoiled rotten" by his older brother and two sisters.

The Family Moves to Haskell

Probably motivated by the hope of finding a better life for their young and growing family, Charlie and Ada Jacks packed their belongings and with their three children, Claude, Una Lee, and Ruth, moved from Bell County, Texas, to Haskell, in Haskell County, Texas. We don't know exactly when this move took place, but its approximate date is apparent. Jimmie's older sister Ruth was born in Belton in 1906. My father, James Martin (Jimmie) Jacks, was born in Haskell on 10 October 1909, so it is clear the family went to Haskell sometime between 1906 and 1909. Things must not have been as bright there as they had hoped. While the 1910 Census shows them in Haskell, we can find evidence that shortly thereafter they returned to Belton. It was in Belton that Jimmie Jacks would attend school, grow to manhood, fall in love, marry Lois Lynn Aldredge, and learn the restaurant business. It would also be in Belton that a tragedy would come, leaving an indelible mark on young Jimmie.

The Belton of Four—Year-Old Jimmie Jacks – 1911-1914

The Belton of my father's early childhood was a distant place from the 21st century we know today. Henry Ford had been making his Model T since 1908 but its $950 price tag and Bell County's mostly unpaved streets and roads insured few Belton residents had one. Telephones were not in every home; medicine by today's standards was primitive. Antibiotics would not be developed for another thirty years. Dr Pepper had been invented, just thirty years earlier 50 miles north in Waco. Jimmie was pampered by his older siblings and often got little treats from their occasional spare change, like a Hershey Bar for two cents or a cold drink for a nickel. He had a choice of not only Coca Cola and Dr. Pepper, but a long list of now extinct "soda waters" to chose from; Tex-A-Cola, Lime Cola, Keen Kola, Cola Hiball, and Nehi Cola would have been just a few. For non-cola choices there would have been Nehi, Whistle, Orange Crush, NuGrape, Grapico, and Cherry Blossoms. I clearly remember when I was about five my father and I were out in the yard looking at a full moon. Most people see a "man in the moon," but my father told me it was really "a bear drinking a Nehi Cola." I could see that bear holding the bottle of soda water in his paws. Now, in my late sixties, it is still easy to remember that night. If only it were still possible to sit out in the back yard and watch that bear in the moon with him today. There are so many more things I would want to tell him. It's funny what your mind chooses to remember. And yes, my children all know about the bear in the moon drinking the Nehi Cola. They say they can see it too.

The Night that Changed Young Jimmie's Life Forever – Wednesday 2 September 1914

It's very possible Ada and her four children, including young Jimmie, heard the shots that rang out about 8:00 p.m. that Wednesday evening. It was dark and the noises of daytime activity and commerce had ceased. Their home, on the banks of Nolan Creek, was only two blocks from the east side of Belton's square where Charlie Jacks had his restaurant. Ada had known of the dispute between Squab Miller and Charlie for a while. The drunks from Miller's saloon next door were walking through Charlie's restaurant, disturbing his customers while they ate. It threatened to ruin his business. We can only wonder about her thoughts when she heard the gun shots.

These were anxious times. Even the average citizen of Belton, seemingly far removed from the conflicts on the European stage, could not help but sense that things were getting much worse. Two months earlier the assassination of Austrian Archduke Francis Ferdinand on June 28 seemed to be pulling the world into some global type of conflict. Newspapers were full of unsettling reports.

Aug 6, Austria-Hungary declared war against Russia and Serbia declared war against Germany

Aug 11, Jews were expelled from Mitchenick, Poland

Aug 12, Great Britain declared war on Austria-Hungary

Aug 19, The British Expeditionary Force (BEF) landed in France

Aug 20, German forces occupied Brussels, Belgium

Aug 22, In France some 27,000 soldiers died in the bloodiest battle of French history

Aug 23, The Emperor of Japan sided with the Allies and declared war on Germany

Aug 25, German troops marched into France and pushed the French army to the Sedan.

Aug 30, The 1st German plane bombed Paris and two people were killed

Sep 1, Russia renamed St. Petersburg to Petrograd

Sep 2, German Zeppelins again bombed Antwerp

Such things dominated conversations, which normally would have centered on how much rain was needed, the price of cotton, and such agriculturally based topics. While the Texas cotton crop looked like a good one (4,384,933 bales), up substantially for the last year's figures, people were nevertheless uneasy about their future. Could all this turmoil unfolding in faraway countries have heightened the tensions on everyone that night? Could drunken patrons of Squab Miller's saloon have goaded him into leaving his bar carrying that pistol, with the purpose of going next door and shooting Charlie Jacks? Had Squab Miller been drinking that night himself? Or had this been a deep-seated seething rage building in him for some time, reaching its climax around 8:00 p.m. that Wednesday evening, 2 September 1914? It's pretty certain we will never know. The sheriff's records can't be located, but the root cause did not change the outcome. Squab Miller would walk into Charlie's restaurant for the purpose of armed confrontation. The confrontation quickly escalated and Squab Miller would shoot Charlie Jacks twice. Several days later those wounds would claim Charlie's life. Young Jimmie Jacks would lose his father before he reached his fifth birthday. This would be the only father-figure he would ever know. It changed his life forever in ways even those close to him will never fully comprehend. And yet, as with everything else in his life, he bore it with true quiet strength and integrity, never allowing it to destroy his ability to show love and tenderness toward those he loved. He never talked about this unimaginable, ever-present inner pain. Perhaps he did to my mother, but certainly not to anyone else. To say "time heals all wounds" is to speak a gross falsehood.

Claude Willis Jacks

Upon Charlie's death, Ada found herself a widow with four children. But God provides . . . even in the midst of tragedy. Ada's oldest son, Claude, was then fifteen. According to my father, there was never any doubt in Claude's mind what his options were; he immediately left school and began working in the restaurant. He became the provider, not only for his mother but for his younger siblings. My father worshiped his big brother Claude. He would say with such affection . . . "that's my bud." Sixty years later when Claude was in a rest home, totally blind, my father would visit him regularly. He would "smuggle" him a cigar which he no longer tried to smoke but would unwrap, smell, and put unlit in his mouth. The nurses all turned a blind eye. He would tenderly hold Claude's hand and they would talk. Jimmie Jacks worshiped his big brother.

Una Lee Jacks

Una Lee was thirteen when Charlie was killed. While still too young to help earn money for the family, she was able to continue her education, thanks to her older brother Claude. Later, with this education she helped support the family by teaching school. The family pulled together to survive. Young Jimmie, while too young to make the sacrifices his older siblings were making, was being impacted in a way which would remain with him forever. Yet, because he internalized this so well, few would ever realize the ever-present pain he carried.

Ruth Nolan Jacks

Only eight when her father died, Ruth helped around the house and helped look after her five-year-old brother Jimmie. Conversations with Ruth decades later would show she was more able to reason through the incident than was her younger brother. In time, Ruth became the de facto family historian. She lived her entire life within a few miles of where she was born, and visited her father and mother's graves frequently. My father was always close to his siblings. This closeness that came about after Charlie Jacks' death unified them throughout their entire lives.

Jimmie and School

To say that my father failed to distinguish himself academically would be somewhat of an understatement. His formal education ended after his sophomore year in high school. While he read well enough, I can remember his asking my mother for help with important letters he was composing in his later years as a manager. He advanced in the workplace due to his relentless work ethic. He worked long and hard and insisted on perfection from himself and those with whom he worked.

Jimmie the Athlete

Jimmie would learn early that he was gifted with athletic ability. His skill on the football field earned him write-ups in newspapers as far away as the *Waco Times Herald*. Jimmie grew up on the banks of Nolan Creek which wound its way through the heart of Belton. The creek bank was in his back yard. As a result he became an expert swimmer and diver. Once when I was about 12, my father stopped by the local Hamilton municipal swimming pool to watch us swim for a few minutes. A group of us had been trying to master a simple jackknife dive. He got out of his pickup and came in. He patiently tried to coach us on how to execute the dive. Finally, he said he would be right back. He returned in a few minutes with his old bathing suit. I'd seen him wearing it in photos but never for real. He put it on and came out to the diving board. He walked straight up to the board, stopped and explained just how and when to open, then marched up on the board, went higher in the air than anybody I'd ever seen, and came down cutting the water like a knife – hardly a ripple. When he came up, he asked us if we had noticed how he held his feet so as to enter the water cleanly. He then proceeded to do a full-gainer, then a half-gainer, all flawlessly, then sat down and explained them to us. After that he went into the dressing room, changed, got back in his pickup and drove off. Aside from being almost speechless after having witnessed a side of my father I had never seen before, I was also bursting with pride. Some of my friends knew I had a cool dad but now everybody at the pool that day knew too.

Another event that sticks out particularly in my memories of his physical skill happened in the heat of summer probably around 1955; a group of us had ridden our bikes down to the Hamilton square. Once there we parked the bikes and were walking around the sidewalks . . . just hanging out. Back then, Hamilton had covered sidewalks. Many of the local businesses had signs painted on what was probably 1x6 boards about 3 feet long, suspended by hooks from the roof that covered the sidewalks. It was an ideal way for pedestrians walking down the sidewalk to easily spot the establishment, rather than waiting till they got to the glass storefronts. Of course it was also ideal for young, energetic, and mischievous boys to run, jump, and slap. Immediately following the slap the signs would make a wonderful whap . . . whap . . . whap . . . sound as they swung violently back and forth dissipating all the energy they had suddenly received from our open handed slap. This athletic achievement in several ways resembled, at least to our young minds, what a hurdle runner in a track meet might experience.

But that day, we slapped the Lone Star Gas Company's sign (my father's office). The idea was, run, jump, slap, and continue running, all the way to the end of that side of the square. Well, at the end of the sidewalk, with several of the signs still swinging in various stages of energy dissipation, as we turned to savor our feat of athletic prowess, we saw my father standing under the Lone Star Gas Company's slowly swinging sign. Our universal conclusion was . . . this is not good. My father motioned with his hand for us to come to him. More than fifty years later, I can still so clearly see him standing there, waiting for us to return; needless to say, a certain state of anxiety existed among us.

He looked down at me and said, "Damn boy, is that the best you can do?" Then he removed the ever-present yellow wooden pencil and notepad from his shirt pocket, removed the loose change from his pants pocket, took off his shoes, stepped one pace back from the sign, jumped in the air, kicked the sign with his feet, then continuing in a back flip landing back on his feet almost where he had begun. He then picked up his loose change, his notepad and pencil, and walked back inside his office.

Our collective thoughts were incongruent with publishing in this family book, but needlessly to say they were all expletives common among adolescent boys in the south. Once again I felt the pride rising in me as I realized everybody knew or would soon know that Jimmy Joe had the coolest dad ever.

Jimmie Meets Lois Lynn Aldredge

She was beautiful, poised, and receiving her education at Baylor College for Women in Belton. Her father had been a Baylor University (Waco) graduate as well as a graduate of the prestigious Southwestern Theological Seminary. Lois' father had died in 1923 when she was only thirteen. Her mother, after the death of her husband, joined the staff at Baylor College for Women. There my mother was required to attend school year round, quickly accumulating university credits far beyond her years. She would later tell me she missed not growing up as "normal girls" did. She had few freedoms and friends.

In 1929, Baylor College for Women had an enrollment of over 2000 students, mostly young women. Jimmie undoubtedly discovered he had acquired an acute interest in at least some aspects of higher education. Visiting with Lois was difficult. Both she and her mother lived on campus. Curfews in this strict Baptist women's college were both rigid and unforgiving, but they managed to meet and soon fell in love. On 22 August 1929, Lois and Jimmie went to Clovis, New Mexico, and were married. They eloped. According to my mother, it was on the occasion of my birth as their first child – some twelve years later – that her mother first spoke to her again.

Following the marriage, they returned to Belton where they lived with Jimmie's mother Ada, while he worked as a waiter and cook in the family restaurant. Ada lived in the house just next to her son Claude and his family, so young Lois acquired a surrogate family. I never learned about the relationship Lois had with her mother-in-law Ada. In some ways it would be very logical that she wanted her own home as soon as possible and thereby was anxious to move out of Ada's home. On the other hand, her relationship with her own mother was severely strained and so it is equally logical Lois and Ada would have become close. Unfortunately, we shall probably never know.

The Great Depression

Within weeks of their marriage the Great Depression officially began, but it was doubtful the newlyweds were paying much attention to financial news. They were in love and Lois was busy learning all about her new family. Even if they had been following stories in the paper during the first few days of their marriage, there was little indication of the economic and personal hard times that lay ahead for most of the nation. Less than two weeks after their marriage, on September 3, 1929, the Dow Jones Industrial Average peaked at 381.17. To the not quite nineteen-year-old bride and her not quite twenty-year-old husband – if they were even aware of it – it could have done nothing but add to their newlywed bliss. But by 29 October . . . only eight weeks later, things began going seriously south. Black Tuesday would command the attention of every breathing adult. The market would lose 13% of its value in one single day. From its high on 3 September until the end of October, the market would lose 40% of its value. The nation was stunned.

Thousands of investors lost large sums of money, and many lost everything. Banks, stores, and factories closed. Massive unemployment was nationwide. Millions of Americans lost their jobs and homes. Many were destitute. Soup kitchens sprang up. Many had to depend on the government or charity for food. Farm and factory life alike was hit. It could have been a very frightening time for the young couple but a miracle spared them the pain the rest of the nation would undergo for the next few years.

Jimmie age 20.

Lois age 16.

Lois Aldredge with mother.

The Lone Star Gas Company

Shortly after all this began, Jimmie was hired by the Lone Star Gas Company and they moved from Belton to Waco. These were happy years for the young couple. With no children and a good job, they enjoyed the circle of friends their own age which Lois had never had growing up. They soon bought a late model car and often took short vacations and weekend getaways to beautiful spots in Texas. A few of these photos survive today. Apparently, picture-taking was something that never interested Jimmie and Lois very much. I remember an old "box camera" that nobody seemed to understand how to operate. On the rare occasions when they would try to use it, almost universally blurry, out-of-focus photos confirmed that taking pictures was not their long suit. With the exception of their favorite stories which would be retold from time to time at gatherings of family and friends, these were the "missing years" in my parent's life together.

Jimmie rose rapidly in the ranks of the Lone Star Gas Company. From ditch-digger to meter reader, then followed shortly by promotion to manager, his career moved quickly. He was first sent to Brenham, Texas. Again these were fun-filled happy years for the young couple. Still with no children and a collie dog named Nip, life was exciting. Not long after that, he was transferred again, this time to McGregor, Texas, as a full sub-sistrict manager. They were on a roll.

McGregor's Beautifully Simple Life —
James Joseph (Jimmy Joe)

It was in McGregor in 1943, after almost twelve years of marriage, that Jimmie and Lois had their first child. He was named James for his father and his great-grandfather on his father's side, and Joseph after Lois's beloved father Rev. Joseph David Aldredge.

Listening To The Radio

In the late 1940s, home life for Lois and Jimmie was beautifully simple. They would sit around their large Philco console radio and listen to that evening's weekly programming. I can still clearly remember hearing the programs and remarkably, remember being interested in the adventure or comedy ones. I don't recall any of the news programs. I remember Lois and Jimmie listening to "The Adventures of Sam Spade" . . . he was a private detective, "The Thin Man," (another private detective I think), "The Inner Sanctum" (which would scare the pants off me with that creaking door sound), "Amos & Andy," "Fibber McGee & Molly" (comedy), and of course, "The Lone Ranger." He was sponsored by Cheerios and I would whine and beg until they bought me a box containing the coupon required to redeem the latest must-have gadget. I don't recall eating them but I can recall watching my mother cut out the coupon and mail it in with some small money taped to it. I would then wait impatiently for the postman to deliver my special Lone Ranger whatever.

Those were wonderful hours playing on the floor between Lois and Jimmie's feet after dinner as they listened to the radio. For some crazy reason I can still recall the program sponsor's advertising. Wild Root Cream Oil (a hair tonic with a catchy jingle . . . . "get Wild Root Cream Oil Charlie" . . . never did find out who "Charlie" was), Philip Morris Cigarettes with the voice of a little hotel bellman saying "Call for Phillip Morris", and the Lava soap ad that went " L-A-V-A --- L-A-V-A" to the beat of timpani drums. I remember crawling behind the huge radio console while it was playing and peering into the back. There was an enormous array of glowing tubes. I can still feel the heat those tubes would generate warming my cheeks as I peered inside.

Jimmie 1943.

Lois 1943.

Camille

It was during this period, in 1948, that their daughter, and last child, Camille was born. Camille was just about the last good thing that would come to Lois and Jimmie in McGregor. Like Jimmy Joe, Camille was born in Hillcrest Hospital in Waco, and was delivered by Dr. C. T. Collins. The electric fans must have been running full speed in all Hillcrest's un-air conditioned rooms. With a high temperature that Thursday of 104 degrees and a low of only 68, plus Camille's birth weight of over 10 pounds, Lois must have been very glad when they placed Camille on her chest.

A Career Setback

Perhaps blinded by how easily their good life had come, Jimmie and Lois took a critical wrong turn. Approached by bankers whom he trusted offering what he naively believed to be a golden opportunity, Jimmie left the Lone Star Gas Company to buy the struggling McGregor Bottling Company. Retrospection would reveal a much different picture than the sellers and bankers presented. While exact details are not available, it is clear the bank was holding some paper which was either non-producing or dangerously close. The bank needed to put a new face and more collateral behind their note. What more perfect way than to pass the debt to a new loan holder with fresh assets? The risky loan would instantly be paid off and disappear from their books, replaced by a new note with a clean history. Though this was a typical banker tactic, my father was too naïve in matters of business to see their ploy until it was too late. The previous owners had neglected to mention a few minor details . . . . the preeminent being Pepsi and Coke were planning on introducing much larger 10 ounce bottles in 1950. McGregor Bottling Company with its 6 ounce bottle – even factoring in the loyal customer base it enjoyed – could never withstand the onslaught.

This later proved to be the stake in the heart for Jimmie and Lois's only venture into the world of business.

I have vague memories of going to the bottling plant while he was working there. I remember another employee staying there late with him. Because of all the machinery in the plant, and my being only five, I wasn't allowed to go often and never free to wander around. I do remember playing out behind the plant where the delivery trucks were parked. I remember not seeing much of him during this period. Jimmie applied the only thing he knew to the problem . . . hard work . . . twelve hour days and seven day weeks. Hard work would prove not enough to save the business, and after a couple of years the plant closed and he returned to Lone Star Gas, but the financial disaster would hang over them for many years to come. They lost the equity in their home in McGregor, and subsequently the bank got a judgment against him. This precluded their being able to own another home for several years. To my father this was a point of shame almost equal to that of how his father had been killed. He always paid his debts and his word was always his bond, but in this case, the debt was an impossible amount. I would be grown before he would again own a home.

Groesbeck

Lone Star Gas graciously offered him a sub-district manager position in Groesbeck. So Jimmie took his wife Lois, five-year-old Jimmy Joe, and infant Camille, and moved the family. The Groesbeck of 1949 was the small rural county seat of Limestone County, with a population of just over 2000, 55 miles east of McGregor and 38 miles east of Waco. Groesbeck owed its existence to the Houston and Texas Central Railway, which passed through the center of town. Groesbeck is remembered today as being the site of Fort Parker where a Comanche attack in 1836 killed five settlers. Five more were captured and 21 eventually managed to escape. The most famous of the captured was a young girl named Cynthia Ann Parker. She later married the Comanche Chief Peta Nocona. One of their children was the famous Comanche Chief Quanah Parker. The actor Joe Don Baker is also a native of Groesbeck.

Groesbeck in 1949 still had deep racial divides. Memories lingered from the turbulent Reconstruction days, fostering poorly-concealed racism. The black people all lived in a separate part of town and went to black schools. The old Groesbeck red brick plant's pit was still a fun place for boys to play. The clay was deep gray and "fools gold" was profusely mixed in the clay. I got my first bicycle while we lived there, and I was allowed to ride it around town. I met friends and started school in Groesbeck. Life was an exciting adventure. A three-pound can of Crisco cost 89 cents; a pound of butter, 68 cents; a one-pound loaf of bread, 14 cents; and a pound of bacon cost 43 cents. Life was beginning to look good for Lois and Jimmie once again.

Hamilton

In the summer of 1952 Lone Star Gas tapped Jimmie for a larger district. Hamilton, the county seat of Hamilton County, Texas, would be their next home. Not only were Lois and Jimmie excited, but this time my sister and I were old enough to understand. Hamilton would be where Camille and I would spend our childhood and adolescence. From here we would become teenagers and later often return as adults. This would be a milestone for all of us. Both Lois and then Jimmie would die and be laid to rest, side by side, here in Hamilton. This was to become "home" for all of us.

"Mayberry"

The Hamilton of 1952 was an almost perfect microcosm. It was almost "Mayberry." Hamilton was first settled in the mid-

1850s. From its early settler days with a population of around 200, it had slowly grown into the 3,080 population county seat of Hamilton County. It had survived the Civil War, Indian raids, the Great Depression, devastating floods, and was about to witness the demise of king cotton. The town had a black population of zero. In the center of its square sat its 1887 county courthouse, built from native limestone. Cotton was already starting to show its decline. While still having three cotton gins, it was a far cry from the five found there in the early 1900s. In late August, the Hamilton night skies glowed orange from the fire and smoke of the cotton gins burning their non-marketable cotton residues.

The square was full of thriving businesses. Hamilton had no large mega-stores and almost all Hamiltonians bought all their food, clothing, and other necessities within a block or two of the square. Their cotton, grain, and livestock were also sold in Hamilton. What goods they needed came from the local merchants or from the Sears, Roebuck and Company mail-order catalog, the Montgomery Ward catalog, or the J. C. Penney catalog. Some of the most affluent might occasionally make the 70-mile drive to Waco and walk the aisles of such department stores as Goldstein-Migel, and Montgomery Ward, but most stayed close to home.

Saturdays

The Saturdays of the early 1950s were days for socializing and shopping. Children were out of school and after early morning chores were done, rural families would come to town to buy supplies for the week and exchange news. At that time, Hamilton had two "picture shows." The Saturday matinee at the Strand Theater cost ten cents and was the perfect place for kids to meet and socialize while their parents were busy at the dry goods and grocery stores. The kids saw great westerns like "The

Cisco Kid," "Roy Rogers," "Zorro," and Lash LaRue. Tarzan, Tarzan and Jane, plus all the wonderful cartoons kept all Hamilton's children entertained on Saturday afternoons while parents shopped. But not long after 4:00 p.m., the square would begin to empty as farm and ranch families headed home to complete the evening chores before dark. For Jimmie and Lois and their young family, Hamilton was a wonderful place to be.

More About Life in "Mayberry"

Gasoline in 1952 cost 28 cents a gallon at Spot Brazil's full service Humble station. As you drove in a bell would ring and at least one attendant would come out, put gas in your car, check your oil level, check all your tire pressures, and clean your windshield. All included in the price of your gas. It cost 3 cents to mail a first class letter. When you wanted to place a telephone call, you picked up the receiver and soon heard the female voice of the telephone operator saying "number please?" Almost everybody was on a "party line." Our phone number was 398-J. We shared the telephone line with the school superintendent whose last name started with W. Their number was 398-W. If you needed to place a call and heard someone talking, you quietly put the receiver back on the hook. It was considered very rude to put it down carelessly as this would make an unpleasant noise for the people already using the line. However, while we never did this, it was considered a last-option protocol to replace the phone in its cradle more firmly, if it became apparent the party using the line was showing flagrant disregard for your need to make a call. Listening in on a call was also considered taboo. Nevertheless, it was well know about town that several old ladies considered listening in to be an entertainment mainstay. Along the same line, another point of humor about town was that as these old ladies became less able to get around, they would diminish the town's telephone system capacity by calling each other first thing in the morning and discussing their latest aches and pains at considerable length. I don't recall anybody ever really getting upset about this . . . it was just considered how things worked in Hamilton.

"High Noon" staring Gary Cooper was playing at the Texan Theater. An actor out in California named Ronald Reagan married an actress named Nancy Davis. Norman Vincent Peale published *The Power of Positive Thinking*. Elizabeth, daughter of King George VI of Britain, became Queen Elizabeth, upon the sudden death of her father. Gibson introduced the Les Paul electric guitar, and Holiday Inn opened their first location in Memphis. The Korean Conflict had been going since 1950 and many brave Hamiltonians served, but for numerous reasons best left to historians to debate, it did not seem so close to home as WWII had. The country was finally on a recovery roll after the hard-time years of the Great Depression followed by WWII.

Jimmie, Lois, Jimmy Joe, and Camille would watch Queen Elizabeth's coronation on their new RCA black and white TV, one of the very first in the neighborhood. When directing people to our house, the easiest way was to say we were the house with the TV antenna. Soon Bert and Fay Schrank, our wonderful neighbors and faithful friends for decades, got one too, so that little bit of elitism didn't last long. Only a couple of years later, people began talking about color TVs. Hamilton certainly didn't have any, but somehow a substitute – a piece of transparent tri-color flexible material showed up in our home. When taped over the TV screen, it gave a ridiculous illusion of a blue sky, unrealistic mid section (people) and a green grass bottom third (even if the bottom of the picture was supposed to be black asphalt). There were moments when our 1950s naiveté was astounding. But that just made life more fun for Jimmie Joe and Camille.

Life in Hamilton for Jimmie was not stressful; even with his responsibilities for managing Lone Star's operations for that area, things moved at a "Mayberry" pace. At noon every day except Sunday, the "Fire Whistle" sounded announcing the lunch hour. Most businesses on the square and elsewhere closed at the sound of the siren and reopened at 1:00 p.m. I remember hearing jokes that it should also sound on Sundays signaling to an overzealous preacher that it was lunchtime for his congregation. Lois and Jimmie met new friends and settled into the Hamiltonian lifestyle. Jimmie joined the local Lions Club. They always had some civic project going and he enjoyed working on them. Lois and Jimmie would soon join the First Baptist Church. Mother was back in the Southern Baptist environment of her childhood. In time, first Jimmy Joe and later Camille would be baptized in that church.

Coffee – A Ritual

Many of the town's businessmen joined together a couple of times each day in what could probably best be described a caffeine-based ritual. Once each morning and usually again in the mid-afternoon, small groups would congregate on the square at City Drug or Jordan Pharmacy or a cafe a few blocks north of the square for sharing coffee, gossip, and opinions. Back then a cup of coffee in Hamilton cost a nickel.

Lois Gets Sick

Life in Hamilton was about to change for Lois and Jimmie. For months Lois had known something was wrong, but like so many women of that era she didn't want to confront her symptoms. Finally, early in January of 1964 she told Jimmie she thought she needed to go see a doctor. For months she had felt tired and often depressed. But, she reasoned, that was probably not all that abnormal for a woman in her early fifties. But then the bloating feelings started, and the pain in her lower back never seemed to go away. Finally her clothes were getting tight around her waist. She knew something in her abdominal area wasn't right. As soon as the doctor saw her he told her she needed to see a specialist. She called Waco and made an appointment with Dr. Collins, the obstetrician and gynecologist who had guided her through both her pregnancies.

Fear gripped them both as they drove the seventy miles from Hamilton to Waco. Jimmie was trying to deal with the situation in the only way he knew. He disguised his fears and turned inward. He was paralyzed with fear almost to the point of silence. He tried hard to conceal his worry but to Lois he was transparent. He was loving and comforting but inside he was probably re-experiencing the emotions of five-year-old Jimmie as his father Charlie Jacks lay bandaged and dying from the two gunshot wounds in his chest. The normally beautiful drive to Waco must have produced few if any comments. Things along Texas Highway 22 from Hamilton to Cranfills Gap, then the Farm to Market back-road into Clifton where they joined Texas Highway 6 on towards Waco, must have gone, for the most part, unobserved.

Hillcrest

In Waco, Dr. C. T. Collins seemed not to offer much reassurance. Surgery was needed now and there was a strong possibility the procedure would not prove a panacea. There were already indications of spreading, even before the laparoscopy. Lois readied herself for the surgery immediately. She summoned her spiritual strength acquired from her beloved father the Rev. Joseph D. Aldredge and her mother Grace Rogers Tyner (she had remarried after Rev. Aldredge died) and moved forward into the fight. Jimmie, while a Christian, did not appear to have such a spiritual reservoir. She was admitted to Hillcrest Hospital (Hillcrest Baptist Medical Center), the same hospital where she had gone to have both Jimmy Joe and Camille. Those were joyous times, but this time . . . things were different.

The old red brick hospital was a Waco institution dating back to 1917. It had an outstanding reputation, it was relatively close to Hamilton, and Dr. Collins – whom she had seen for years – practiced there. Lois would have her surgery and go into room 416-A to recover. Few hospitals in Texas could have matched the surgical and nursing skills offered by Hillcrest. But in Lois's case this would turn out not to be enough. According to Dr. Collins, the ovarian cyst he removed was the size of a grapefruit and ruptured during the surgical procedure, dumping cancerous cells into her abdominal cavity. While this in itself is quite serious, its influence on the eventual outcome was probably inconsequential. The cancer had already begun its metastasis, spreading from the ovary into the abdominal cavity, the diaphragm, stomach, colon, and probably her liver. Her abdomen already had a distended, thick, hard feeling. Her doctors estimated she had three to twelve months to live. She would live only three.

Twilight Comes to "Mayberry"

In most ways, the hospital stay was the best part of the ordeal for Lois. All their family friends were told she could not receive visitors, but this all ended when she returned home to Hamilton. The house was a steady stream of visitors, from just good-hearted well-wishers, to loving neighbors and church members. It wasn't hard to spot the curious as well. But along with this flow of Hamiltonians and relatives came endless amounts of food. In rural Texas towns, when one was sick, friends and neighbors brought food. Jimmie, on the surface, appeared to enjoy all the people, but I'm really quite sure it was a defense mechanism. Among the throngs was what I could classify as real saints from the First Baptist Church and other churches as well. They were real prayer warriors. They prayed with amazing dedication for her to recover.

A momentary bright spot for Lois in the midst of all this was getting to play with her first grandchild, Jason Jerome. While she soon became too weak to carry him, and while he was not yet walking, he would play on her bed and she would watch in loving amazement at his expressions. As I held him upright for her, my heart was breaking knowing this would be all she would ever get to see – not even his first steps or his first words. As she cooed and tickled him, I could see moments of sadness passing across her face as she too realized the truth of the moment. She would not live to see him reach his ninth month.

It wasn't long before the ravages of the rapidly spreading cancer were beginning to make it clear to Lois where this path would lead. Later in our long talks she revealed her acceptance of the ultimate outcome, though she feared the intense pain she rightly expected to endure. Occasionally, in her most candid moments she would show brief lapses in her courage about facing that ultimate moment. She wondered if it would be like walking toward the light, stepping across, or just darkness and nothing. I learned a lot about the process that intelligent, aware people go through as they approach that unique, yet shared moment in everyone's life. I fully expect, if given the opportunity as the moment looms, to experience the same thoughts and anxieties my mother, Lois Lynn Aldredge Jacks did, as she neared her own mortality.

James R. McDonald – ("Little Jimmy")

During this time, her nephew, "Little Jimmy" came and stayed several weeks. He was the son of my father's oldest sister, Una Lee, and was named after my father. Jimmy was much older than I, and had a successful career in acting, modeling, and the corporate world. About three years earlier he had moved permanently to Milan, Italy, and had come home for a few months vacation to be with his mother and Lois. He brought Una Lee to visit, then took her back home to Fort Stockton, Texas, and returned immediately to Hamilton to be with Lois. He was very devoted to both his mother and my mother. He loved my mother as he loved his own. He paid lots of attention to Lois, they would talk for hours. While she was in the hospital, he remodeled our living room, adding many things and reupholstering all the chairs in perfect coordination. His sense of style, form, and art were truly amazing. Mother was so surprised when she saw her new living room. I was away in the Navy at the time and will forever be grateful to "Little Jimmy" for the love he showed my mother.

The Hamilton Hospital

Her pain started getting worse . . . much worse. Dr. Don McCord began coming to the house and giving her injections to help her tolerate the pain. In her last days, she became so weak, drifting in and out of consciousness, that it became necessary to admit her to the Hamilton hospital, solely to insure her last hours were as comfortable as possible. She was no longer able to tolerate any food by mouth. Hallucinations began occurring at this time too. Finally the doctors began the administration of intravenous paraldehyde, rendering her almost completely unconscious. The family made the decision that she would never be left alone in the hospital. Someone sat with her the entire time. My father, Camille, close family friends Fay and Bert Schrank, and my grandmother, Grace Aldredge, all kept watch over her during these last hours.

My "Vision"

On my night to stay with her, I sat with my chair close to her bed so I could try to hold her hand. That was difficult as she was quite restless from the hallucinations. At one time I put my head on her bed and was resting when I apparently drifted off to sleep. I would estimate the time to have been around 2:30 a.m. to 3:00 a.m. During this sleep, I heard Mother's voice calling me. She was calling my name over and over . . . . "Jimmy Joe . . . Jimmy Joe." I awoke and raised my head. There was a silver-hued gentle glow above us. I could hear her calling me and the voice was coming from the light above us . . . not from her peacefully resting body in the bed. I said "Where are you?" And my Mother's voice replied so clearly . . . "I'm in the air . . . I'm everywhere." The light then went away and I found myself sitting beside her bed staring into her resting face. The hair on the back of my neck and on my arms was standing up. I instantly thought she might have just died, but as I reached out and touched her hand it was warm and she was breathing normally . . . something she did not always do in those last hours. She looked so at peace. For me, sleep did not return that night. I alertly watched as the sun's rays began to bring light to the darkness of that Saturday, May 8th morning, around 5:45 a.m. But as others began to arrive in her hospital room, it seemed as though all the energy in my body suddenly left. I remember being so tired I could hardly speak. I told no one about this experience. I went back to my parents' house, where I would immediately fall into an extremely deep sleep.

The End

It was while I was there sleeping that she quietly slipped away. She was surrounded by two close friends, her mother, Jimmie, and Camille. They would call from the hospital, some-how awakening me from what was probably the deepest sleep of my life, saying I needed to come to the hospital right away. She was already gone but they didn't want to tell me on the phone. As I walked in the room she was still in the bed, her face uncovered. She appeared to be sleeping. My grandmother sat stoically in the corner. Her Bible was in her lap. All others stood around quietly allowing me to have my last moments with my mother. I approached her bed, took her already cold hand in mine, kissed it, and walked out of the room. I was totally oblivious to the social obligations I owed to the others in the room.

There are many moments in my life I would like the opportunity to relive differently. This is one of those. I remember being angry with my grandmother for not showing any more emotion than she did. Just sitting there in that straight-back chair with her Bible in her lap. As my spiritual faith grew, I would come to realize that what I saw was the faith of a saint. Thank God I didn't express this anger directly toward her. I walked from mother's hospital room, got in my new 1964 Ford Mustang, pushed the gas pedal to the floor and experience the car's full acceleration for the first time. Its 289-cubic inch (4.7 liter) V-8 engine seemed to explode. As the tires gained traction, I turned the radio to full volume. "Stop In The Name of Love" by the Supremes came blaring out at me. I hated that group and I hated that song. While I can't remember the exact stream of expletives that instantly flooded my mind, I remember clearly that they did. I did not decelerate (stop) until I reached Highway 36. There were so many good songs during that period, from the British Invasion to Sam Cooke, The Beach Boys, Marvin Gaye, The Righteous Brothers . . . why couldn't just one be playing on one of the small handful of stations that could be received in Hamilton's reception area. I waited at the stop sign just long enough to take advantage of a slight opening in the traffic, then turned left and pushed the accelerator to the floor once more. This time the Mustang fishtailed before finally gaining traction. Upon reaching the "Y" where Texas Highway 22 splits off from Highway 36 just by what was then Truck Town, I veered left and went out Hwy 22 as far as the City Lake.

There I pulled off the road and just sat there for a while. My mind was racing as I tried to grasp what changes I might face in life with one of my parents, the woman who brought me into the world, now gone.

Lois Lynn Aldredge Jacks went to be with the Lord on Saturday, 8 May, 1965 about 11:30 a.m. She came into the world and she left the world on a Saturday. She was just 54 years old. Jimmie was without the love of his life for the first time since he was twenty years old. It would be impossible to grasp the depth of his loneliness.

Lois's Funeral

Since the funeral would be a large one, and since the family was all here or very close, it was decided to hold the funeral service the following day in order to cause the least disruption to those wishing to attend. So on Sunday, 9 May 1965, in the First Baptist Church, a huge portion of the town came together in the mid-afternoon to celebrate her life and help the family and close friends mourn. Rev. Ray Burdett, her former pastor, who came back from Austin and Rev. Mac Hargrove, her present pastor, conducted the service.

The casket was open and she was so remarkably beautiful and appeared to finally be resting so peacefully. At her request they were playing Claude Debussy's "Clair de Lune," "Liebestraum" by Franz Liszt, and "Take My Hand Precious Lord." And of course "Amazing Grace." I can't remember if she had also requested that one but I suppose it really didn't matter as virtually no Baptist funeral can conclude without "Amazing Grace." As I recall, "Clair de Lune" and "Liebestraum" raised some eyebrows amongst some of Hamilton's church folks of 1965. Classical music was not quite what they were accustomed to hearing from the pews in Hamilton in the mid-1960s, but all realized it was in perfect character for Lois and all were graciously understanding. And she would probably have appreciated the irony . . . her funeral was on Mother's Day.

Afterward, at the graveside services, cars stretched southward along the east side of Highway 281 for almost half a mile. It was a beautiful late spring day. There was a tiny trace of rain with basically beautiful skies and temperatures just over 80 degrees. The cemetery plot Jimmie had selected had an oak tree on it. He knew Lois would want a spot with trees. A month later, I would purchase the lot adjoining theirs directly to the north. It was important to me then, as it is now, to know I will someday rest beside my mother and father.

Life After Lois

Mother had a dog named Sheba, of course from the 1952 movie "Come Back Little Sheba," starring Burt Lancaster and Shirley Booth. Before Lois's death Jimmie hadn't paid all that much attention to the dog, but after mother died, it seemed he never put her down. She was always in his lap and he would gently stroke her head. He missed Lois so much. I would watch him sit in front of the television with Sheba in his lap; gently stroking her, and I would have to leave the room in tears.

Camille wasn't quite 17 when Lois died. It was the spring of her junior year at Hamilton High School. But in just over a year, her life would move forward as she left Hamilton for college. Jimmie and Sheba would remain in the large empty house in front of the TV. He and Sheba watched the "Beverly Hillbillies," "Perry Mason," "The Munsters," and "Rawhide." And of course there was the "Tonight Show with Johnny Carson." I always figured that when Sheba died, it would be from lung cancer caused by second-hand cigarette smoke emanating from the ever-present cigarette in Jimmie's hand or the ever-present heavy glass ash tray at his feet.

The Decline of Jimmie's Health

For some time Jimmie had been noticing he was getting short of breath. As he worked, it became necessary for him to stop and catch his breath more often. Going to see a doctor was something against his nature, like admitting some kind of failure in being unable to tough out whatever it was that he had. My father was rarely sick and I only remember his seeing a doctor on a couple of occasions while I was growing up. So certainly by the time he had decided to seek a doctor's advice, his emphysema (COPD) was well advanced. I'm not really sure that would prove to be a significant factor in his prognosis, but it could have allowed his medical retirement from Lone Star Gas much sooner. The disease had no cure and little meaningful treatment except the use of oxygen. Dr. Don McCord diagnosed his condition on his first office visit. As Jimmie would later recount, Dr. McCord had just purchased this new diagnostic device which measured the pressure one could exert when blowing into it. Jimmie's test pressures were so low that they left no question concerning his lung condition. Jimmie would leave Don McCord's office that day with a letter diagnosing him with pulmonary emphysema and stating he was no longer able to work. Less than a week later he was medically retired. While smoking since he was ten years old probably was the primary contributor, there is little question that working around the fumes of natural gas most of his adult life with complete disregard to any possible medical consequence couldn't have helped. I never recall seeing any type of mask they were required to wear, but knowing my father, even if there had been one, he would not have worn it.

Jimmie's Retirement

In many ways, Jimmie seemed to be happier in retirement than he was while working. Perhaps the physical demand as his lung capacity diminished was greater than any of us knew. But whatever the reason, Jimmie enjoyed his retirement. He could now spend as much time as he wanted in the coffee shop visiting with his friends. Also, for the first time in my memory, he developed a circle of friends – basically his coffee drinking buddies. They had a gang that would go to all the Hamilton Bulldog High School football games. Perhaps some in the gang invited him out of kindness after seeing the loneliness that enveloped his life when Lois died.

Jimmie's life, while now free from the structure previously imposed by his work, was ordered by his own design. He loved his new routines. In the fall, Fridays were for high school football with the guys and Sundays were for the Dallas Cowboys. Every Wednesday he would drive to Fort Worth where I was in flight school. He would spend the night with us and leave for Hamilton on Thursday morning. He enjoyed the drive and he enjoyed playing with his only grandchild, Jason.

It was, however, gradually becoming noticeable to everyone that he was losing the ability to do even the slightest physical task without becoming exhausted. Use of his ever-present oxygen bottle was increasing. He remained mobile and continued in his activities, but he needed ever-increasing pauses to allow him to catch his breath. Watching this once superior athlete deteriorate was hard for us. It also caused me to speculate about what the latter years of my life might be like. A rare thought process for a 24-year-old Jimmy Joe.

Jimmie Remarries

Jimmie's life in many ways was pleasant, but the reality of coming home to the large empty house without his beloved Lois was ever-present. For many years Jimmie had known Viola Robinson and her husband. Several years earlier Viola's husband had died. Viola had always worked in the cafes where Jimmie drank coffee. Their friendship grew over the years and eventually led to romance. On 30 March 1972, seven years after Lois died, Jimmie and Viola were married in a small private ceremony. Jimmie moved into Viola's house and closed down his home.

The Spotted Horse

Soon afterwards, Viola and Jimmie decided to open a restaurant of their own. Vi had always worked in a restaurant or cafe and Jimmie grew up in one. It was a very natural move. While Jimmie's emphysema prevented him from doing much physically, his keen eye for how things should be was a great help. They bought the struggling Spotted Horse Restaurant and rapidly turned it into the place to eat in Hamilton.

With the money they were making from the restaurant and with a few key trusted employees, Vi and Jimmie were able to take a few days off each month. They would regularly visit his brother Claude and his sister Ruth. Claude still lived in Belton and Ruth lived in Temple about 10 miles from Belton. They also found time to travel out of town for dinner with some of their Hamilton friends. Jimmie loved people and he loved eating out. So once again Jimmie was happy. Even sitting at the family table at the Spotted Horse was enjoyable for him. He once more had a life outside the large empty house.

The End

While Jimmie's life was happier than he had been since Lois got sick, his health continued to get worse. He was coughing more and more as his lungs continued to lose their elasticity. He had to struggle to keep enough oxygenated air in his lungs. This caused frequent prolonged coughing spells. One afternoon he had to leave the restaurant and go back home due to his coughing. While at home alone, he suddenly became dizzy and began

losing consciousness. He fell to the floor. Eventually he was able
to crawl to the phone and dial the Spotted Horse. Vi rushed
home. It was evident Jimmie was in very serious condition. He
was rushed to the Hamilton Hospital, where they quickly determined he was bleeding internally. They rushed him to Temple to
Scott & White Hospital and rushed him immediately into
surgery. The doctors found what they had expected; a ruptured
aorta. His chest cavity was filled with blood. He was near death.
The surgeons repaired the aorta and sent him to intensive care.
In a normal person, this would have marked the beginning of an
almost certain complete recovery. However, in Jimmie's case,
with his now weak physical condition and his lungs weakened
by emphysema, he could not resume breathing on his own. He
remained on the respirator.

Camille sent an urgent telegram to Saudi Arabia telling me
to come home immediately. For whatever reason, the first
message did not arrive. A more frantic message arrived the
following day. This one was delivered by a driver accompanied
by a message from the Special Flight Division of Saudi Arabian
Airlines (my employer) advising that our tickets were being
prepared and to pack for immediate departure. The flight home
from Jeddah was a long one. About seven hours to London, then
making less than perfect connections on to New York, then
connecting again in New York for Dallas-Fort Worth, where we
were met by family members and driven on immediately to
Temple.

When we arrived Jimmie was unconscious. He really never
regained awareness from the time he entered surgery. We slept at
Ruth's house and spent the days at the hospital. But it was
becoming clear to everyone that he was too weak to recover. I
remembered from my medical training in the military that in a
deeply unconscious person nearing death, the hearing is one of
the last senses to go. I was sure he could hear us. My wife was

pregnant with Marty. I remember holding his hand and whispering in his ear that she was going to have a baby. I felt his finger twitch. I was completely sure he heard what I said and he summoned his last energy to respond.

My jetlag was passing over me like a black veil. I went to the little lounge adjacent to the critical care ward. There was a family from Hamilton in the lounge. Actually I had gone to school with the man and knew his wife also. I tried to talk to them but I was too tired. I excused myself and lay halfway stretched out on the couch, and was immediately in a deep sleep. The next thing I remember was someone gently shaking my shoulder trying to wake me. It was like trying to climb out from a deep well. Amazing as I look back now . . . the same situation as when my mother died and the phone's endless ringing until I finally managed to sit up. They were telling me I needed to go to my father's room immediately. I assumed he was rapidly slipping away. I rushed to his room still fighting the fog of my jetlag's deep sleep. As I rushed past the nurses' station, I noticed they were all watching me unnaturally. The door to his room was closed. As I opened the door I saw the sheet pulled over his head. The nurses had already removed his IV. I walked slowly to the bed and gently pulled the sheet back. He lay there as though in a peaceful sleep. I took his hand. It was losing body temperature but still not cold. Strong emotions were swirling around me. My father was now gone. I was horribly sad. I loved him so much. I gently placed his hand back on the bed beside him and covered his face again. This time I walked out in a daze. This time there was no compulsion to flog a Ford Mustang. I was so drained I could hardly walk or talk. As I left the hospital to return to Aunt Ruth's house, the early October sun shown warmly on my face. The temperature was almost 80 degrees. The sky was cloudless. Under other circumstances . . . a perfect day.

My father, James Martin Jacks, was born on Sunday 10 October 1909. He died on his 67th birthday, Sunday, 10 October 1976. In the following months, I experienced a strange and illogical fear. I would equate it to something a small child might experience as a result of being separated from its parents in a large store. My father, while always there for support, hadn't really done anything for me physically or materially for many years . . . and yet . . . I felt afraid and alone. I suppose it was just knowing he was always there. In time, the feelings passed and only warm wonderful memories of love and appreciation now remain. Jimmie rests beside Lois in Hamilton's Oakwood Cemetery.

Jimmieisms

My father was full of colloquial expressions. Most probably he was exposed to these as a child growing up in Belton. It seemed I was always doing something that triggered one. For example, when I was being somewhat less that graceful, he would say . . . "Boy, you look like a bull in a china closet."

When he thought I was just selling out and going along with the crowd, he'd say "Boy, you always try to drink upstream of the herd."

When he thought I was making a foolish purchase or taking an unnecessary risk with my hard-earned money . . . usually with the excuse that this purchase would "really" save me money . . . he would say . . . "Boy, the quickest way to double your money is to fold it over and put it back in your pocket."

If I was doing really well at something he'd say, "Boy, you're in high cotton," with the emphasis on a drawn-out pronunciation of "hiiiiigh." Or another favorite was, "Boy, you're ridin a gravy train with biscuit wheels."

When something was hard to come by, it would always be "scarce as hen's teeth."

If I was being lazy he'd say "Boy . . . . nobody ever drowned in sweat."

When something good came to me without my having done anything of particular worth to deserve it or I just got lucky on something he would say . . . "Even a blind hog can find an acorn once in a while."

And finally, when it appeared I'd made some kind of social blunder (not unheard of) he would say "Boy . . . you can cut off a dog's tail . . . but you can't sew it back." How true. But I found that after a while you more or less got used to looking at the bob-tailed dog and it didn't look nearly as bad as it did at first.

Over the years, I've dutifully passed most of these on to my children. When I hear them use one, I always feel just a little bit closer to my father. I hope these "Jimmieisms" will live on in my children's children as my father's fathers have lived on in me.

AFTERWORD

After completing the main body of my work, I was surprised
by the transformation I'd personally undergone. While growing
up, I'd respected my father immensely but was always aware he
was just one of the many ordinary hard-working middleclass
citizens of Hamilton County, Texas. I was vaguely aware his
father, my grandfather, had owned a cafe and had been killed in
a gunfight. Again, just another ordinary hard-working middleclass citizen, except perhaps for the unfortunate bit of unwanted
notoriety of having lost his life in a gun fight. Likewise I knew
my great-grandfather had been an ordinary Arkansas red-dirt
farmer whose only notoriety might have been the fact he had
seventeen children and two step-children. I recalled being told
my 2nd great grandfather had fought for the Confederacy in the
Civil War. For me, it had all ended there. The possibility that I
might have had a Revolutionary War ancestor (much less
several) never crossed my mind.

Today I am a member of Sons of Confederate Veterans. My
application to Sons of the American Revolution is submitted,
and I can't wait for an opportunity to tell anyone willing to
listen about the Jacks family's long history in America.

FOR FURTHER READING

Had I included all the interesting facts I ran across while researching the background of each individual generation, the pages of this book would have been as numerous as the grains of sand on a beach. Nevertheless, I found this background information so interesting that I could not finish the book without leaving some suggestions for further reading.

Sons of Confederate Veterans
P.O. Box 59
Columbia, TN 38402
1-800-MY-DIXIE
http://www.scv.org/

National Society Sons of the American Revolution
1000 South Fourth Street
Louisville, Kentucky 40203-3208
(P) 502-589-1776 | (F) 502-589-1671
http://www.sar.org/

National Society Daughters of the American Revolution
1776 D Street, NW
Washington, D.C. 20006-5303
(202) 628-1776
http://www.dar.org/

Ancestry.com
http://www.ancestry.com/

The Church of Jesus Christ of Latter-day Saints
Family History Library
35 N. West Temple Street, Room 344
Salt Lake City, Utah 84150-3440
801-240-2584
http://mormon.org/family-history

Early Marriages in Bath County, Kentucky
Bonds 1811 – 1850 and Returns 1811 – 1852
Paul McClure
Heritage Books, Inc.

The Library of Samford University
800 Lakeshore Drive
Birmingham, AL 35229
Contains numerous early Jefferson County Alabama resources.
Of special interest is RUHAMA, The Story of a Church 1819 –
1945 by Thomas E. Huey, © 1946 Ruhama Baptist Church,
Birmingham. Alabama.

Pine Bluff / Jefferson County Library System
Main Library – Reference Dept.
200 East Eighth Ave.
Pine Bluff AR 71601-5092
870-534-4802
www.pbjclibrary.org

Chickasaw County Historical & Genealogical Society, Inc.
PO Box 42
Houston, MS 38851
History of the Westward Movement
Frederick Merk
Alfred A. Knopf – New York 1978

Boone, a Biography
Robert Morgan
A Shannon Ravenel Book
Algonquin Books of Chapel Hill 2007
P.O. Box 2225
Chapel Hill, NC 27515-2225

Who Do You Think You Are?
[Encyclopedia of Genealogy]
Nick Barratt
Harper Collins Publishers
77-85 Fulham Palace Road
Hammersmith, London W6 8JB
www.harpercollins.co.uk

A Peoples History of the American Revolution
How Common People Shaped the Fight for Independence
Ray Raphael
A New Press People's History
The New Press, New York, New York

The Encyclopedia of Arkansas History & Culture Project
Encyclopedia of Arkansas
Central Arkansas Library System
100 Rock St.
Little Rock, AR 72201

Engagement at Jenkins' Ferry
http://www.encyclopediaofarkansas.net/encyclopedia/entry-
detail.aspx?entryID=1136

Archives of Maryland Online
http://www.msa.md.gov/megafile/msa/speccol/sc2900/sc2908/ht
ml/index.html
History of Annapolis
City of Annapolis MD
http://www.ci.annapolis.md.us/Visitors/History.aspx

www.ingramcontent.com/pod-product-compliance
Lightning Source LLC
Chambersburg PA
CBHW020449100426
42813CB00026B/3011